Student's Book

Pathway to Science 1

CB078481

Glue your picture here.

Name

Richmond

To discover the world around us we use our...

Scientific Research Skills

Richmond
St Aldates
ford
1 1ST
ited Kingdom

thway to Science Student's Book Level 1

st Edition: 2014
urth Reprint: March 2015
BN: 978-607-06-0904-6

ithway to Science 1 is a collaborative work, created and designed by e Department of Educational Research of Santillana.
Richmond Publishing, S.A. de C.V. 2014
/. Río Mixcoac No. 274, Col. Acacias,
enito Juárez, C.P. 03240, Ciudad de México

ublisher: Justine Piekarowicz
ditor: Dominic Wright
rt and Design Coordinator: Marisela Pérez
re-Press Coordinator: Daniel Santillán

lustrations: Álvaro de la Vega Arancibia, Digital Stuff

'hotographs: César Vargas Ulloa
REPOSITORIO: Santillana Educación S.L. p. 34 (MATTON-
ILD); ©THINKSTOCK: AbleStock.com p. 155; Digital Vision p.
5 (Nick White); Hemera p. 96 (Andrii Andrieiev); iStock pp. 12
Entwicklungsknecht, humbak), 24 (Steve Byland), 43 (paitoonphoto),
8 (s_derevianko, anna1311), 67 (claudiodivizia, fotoedu), 73 (Anton
'rado PHOTOGRAPHY), 96 (Dax Clinkscale), 103 (Viktor Fischer), 139
ksushsh), 155 (sjallenphotography, SylvieBouchard, Jan Will, Christian
Ausat), 157 (sugar0607, jswax, pkh106, John Nielsen, Cheryl Davis,
rina Drazowa-Fischer), 159 (Feng Yu), (shalamov); Photos.com
op. 67 (Jupiterimages), 155 (Jupiterimages), 157 (Jupiterimages),
159 (Hemera Technologies); Stockbyte. p. 65 (Jupiterimages), 157
(Comstock, John Foxx, Thinkstock); p. 138 (Design Pics)
Cover Design: Erika Martínez
Cover Photograph: iStock (Zurijeta), Dandelion seed outdoors

First published by Santillana del Pacífico S.A. de Ediciones

Printed in Brazil by Forma Certa Gráfica Digital
Lote: 808130
Codigo: 292709046 / 2025

Introduction

Hi friends!

We are **Spot**  and **Kiki** , and we are here to welcome you to **Pathway to Science**. Follow this pathway to a very special place. Do you want to know why it is so special?

- It is full of magic, and everyone is welcome in it. You will find information, texts, pictures and activities presented in a simple and friendly manner. Here you will discover that learning is fun!
- This is a space where we can all learn to share and live together. The activities will help us reflect on our values and learn to respect others.

- It is open to people from all over the world, a place where you can continue to learn more and interactively with the help of the latest technology.
- It is filled with challenges that involve finding solutions, developing math skills and applying calculation strategies that you and your classmates will work on together.

We will be with you every step of the way!
All you need is curiosity and the desire to learn.

How is your textbook organized?

Pathway to Science 1 is organized into five units. Here is what you will find in each unit.

Initial Pages

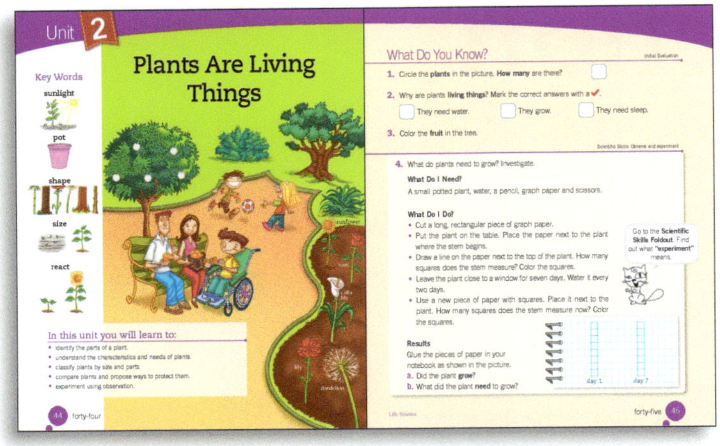

- Number and title of the unit
- Learning objectives
- Initial evaluation

Organized into Sections

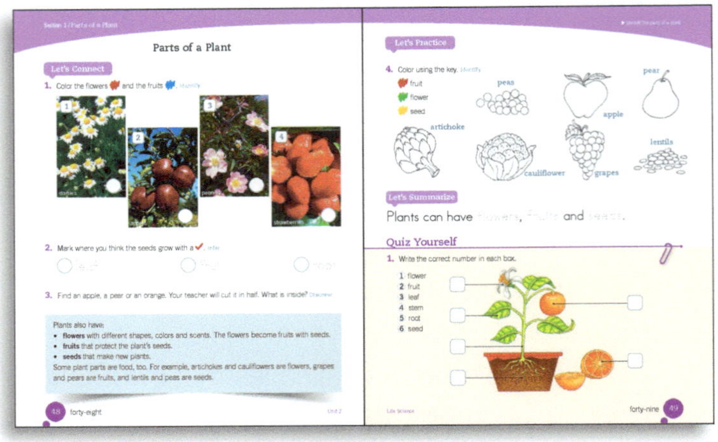

- Let's Connect
  Observe, read, explore and discuss.
- Let's Practice
- Let's Summarize
- Quiz Yourself

Fun Features

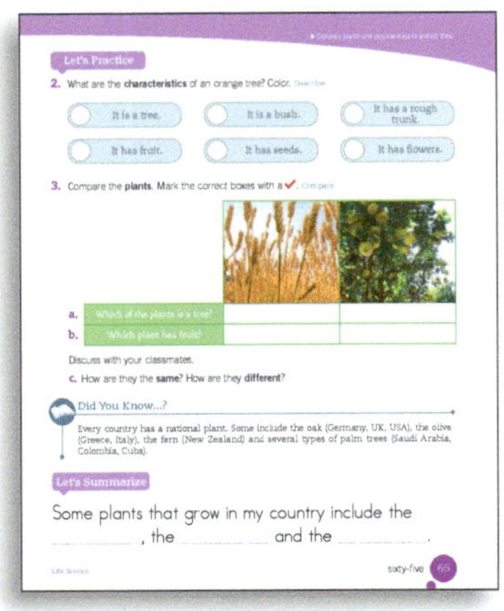

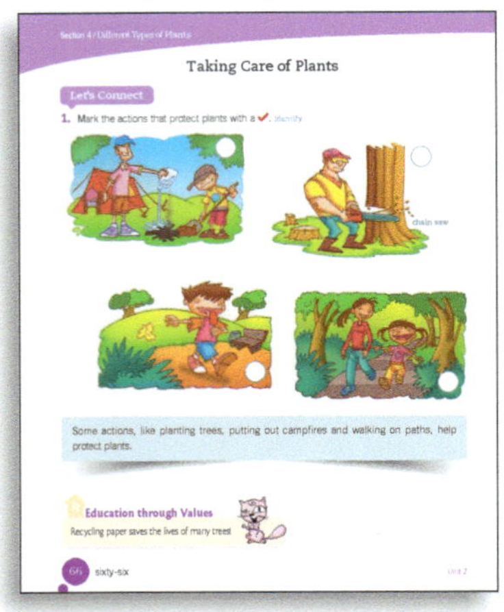

- Education through Values
- Staying Healthy
- Did You Know...?
- Tip
- Word Focus
- Fun Fact!
- Challenge

Evaluation Pages

- What Do You Know?
  Initial Evaluation
- Let's Check!
  Intermediate Evaluation
- What Did You Learn?
  Final Evaluation

Special Pages

- Science Lab
- Test Study Pages
  Summary and Review

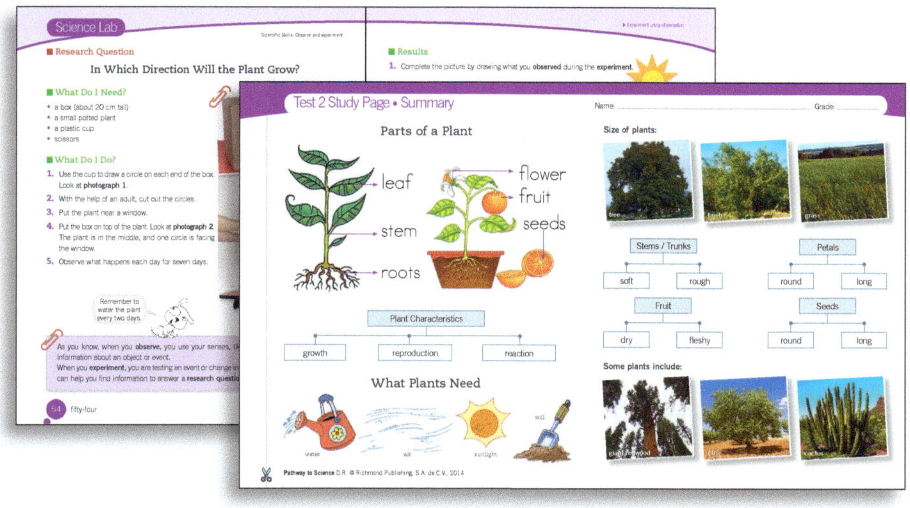

Support Pages

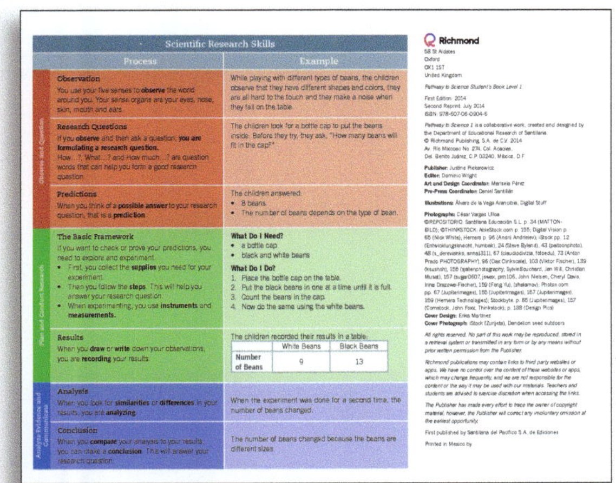

- Scientific Skills Foldout
- Cutouts
- Stickers
- Activity Cards

Table of Contents

Section 5	Section 6	Science Lab	Evaluations	Summary and Review
Classifying Animals **Education through Values:** respecting living things pg. 32	Different Types of Animals **Education through Values:** taking care of the planet pg. 38	What Makes a Living Thing Alive? pg. 18	What Do You Know? Initial Evaluation pg. 9 Let's Check! Intermediate Evaluation pg. 30 What Did You Learn? Final Evaluation pg. 42	Test 1 Study Page
		In Which Direction Will the Plant Grow? pg.54	What Do You Know? Initial Evaluation pg. 45 Let's Check! Intermediate Evaluation pg. 62 What Did You Learn? Final Evaluation pg. 68	Test 2 Study Page
		How Do Different Foods Taste? pg. 82	What Do You Know? Initial Evaluation pg. 71 Let's Check! Intermediate Evaluation pg. 84 What Did You Learn? Final Evaluation pg. 92	Test 3 Study Page
		Can I Make a Toy? pg. 114	What Do You Know? Initial Evaluation pg. 95 Let's Check! Intermediate Evaluation pg. 106 What Did You Learn? Final Evaluation pg. 116	Test 4 Study Page
		How Does Sunlight Affect Daily Activities? pg. 132	What Do You Know? Initial Evaluation pg. 119 Let's Check! Intermediate Evaluation pg. 126 What Did You Learn? Final Evaluation pg. 134	Test 5 Study Page

Unit 1

Animals Are Living Things

Key Words

eat

care for

feed

grow

move

In this unit you will learn to:

- compare and contrast living things and nonliving things.
- recognize the characteristics and needs of living things.
- classify and compare animals according to their habitats and how they move.
- compare animals according to their feeding and reproductive processes.
- compare animals according to number of feet, size and body covering.
- learn about and compare animals of the world.
- observe characteristics of living things.

What Do You Know? Initial Evaluation

1. Look at the picture. Circle the **living things** in red.
2. Look at the picture. Circle the **objects** in blue.
3. Go to **Sticker Set 1** on **page 155**. Stick the animals on the picture.

Scientific Skill: Observe

4. Let's work like scientists! Look at the seagull.

- What is the seagull doing? Mark the correct answer with a ✔.

☐ The seagull is eating.

☐ The seagull is sleeping.

Section 1

Living Things and Nonliving Things

Is It Alive or Not?

Let's Connect

1. Look at the picture. Color the correct answers. Identify

	Alive	Not Alive
a. the boy	○	○
b. the birds	○	○
c. the water	○	○

Plants, animals and people are **living things**.

There are things that are not alive all around us. We call these **nonliving things**.
In the environment, there are natural nonliving things, like rocks and water. There are nonliving things created by people, too. Toys and buildings are examples of nonliving things.

Let's Practice

2. Which of these are living things? Color the **living things**. Identify

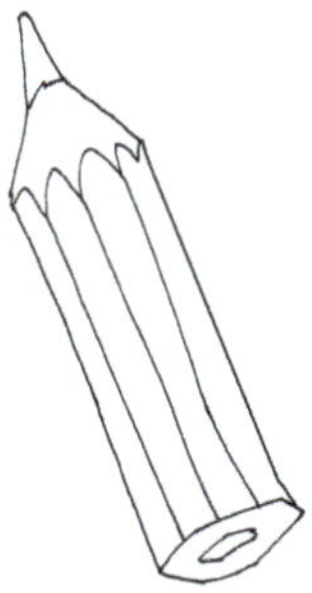

3. Go to **Cutout 1** on **page 143**. Glue the living things and the nonliving things in the correct boxes. Classify

living things	nonliving things

Let's Summarize

Living things are people, animals and plants.
Things that are not alive are called **nonliving things**.

Word Focus

The **environment** is everything that is around people and animals.

The Difference between Animals and Objects

Let's Connect

1. Look at the pictures. Mark the correct answers with a ✔. Compare and contrast

- ◯ It moves.
- ◯ It eats.
- ◯ It breathes.

- ◯ It moves.
- ◯ It eats.
- ◯ It breathes.

Fun Fact!

Both pigeon parents take care of their eggs.

How are the bird and the rock different?

2. Complete the sentences. Conclude

- The  is a living thing.
- The  is a nonliving thing.
- The  and  are different.

Plants, animals and people are **different** from **nonliving things**. For example, a bird needs food and a rock does not.

Challenge

How else are living things and nonliving things different? Name two more similarities and two more differences.

Let's Practice

3. Look at the pictures.

a. Mark the correct answers with a ✓. Compare and contrast

It moves by itself.		
It grows.		
It is a living thing.		
It is a nonliving thing.		

b. What happens if the boat does **not** have batteries? Circle the correct picture. Predict

Let's Summarize

Living things and nonliving things are different.

Quiz Yourself

1. Mark the correct answer with a ✓.

A The boy is similar to the boat. They both eat and breathe.

B The boy and the boat are different. The boy eats and breathes, and the boat does not.

Section

2 Living Things

Characteristics of Living Things

Let's Connect

1. Look at the pictures. Mark the correct answers with a ✓. Identify

Word Focus

A **characteristic** is something distinct about a person, place or thing.

		yes	no
a.	Do all living things **grow**?		
b.	Can all living things **have babies**?		
c.	If you get close to a pigeon, will it **fly away**?		

Living things have several characteristics: **they grow**, **they reproduce** and **they react**.

Let's Practice

2. What happens **before** and **after**? Write 1, 2 or 3 next to the correct picture. Put in order

3. What happens in each situation? Guess and mark with a ✔. Predict

What do you do when it is **cold**?

What happens if you **touch** a snail's tentacle?

Let's Summarize

Characteristics of Living Things

- growth
- reproduction
- reaction

Needs of Living Things

Let's Connect

1. Look at the pictures. Answer the questions. Predict

   a. If you put seeds next to a bird and a piece of wood, which of the two will eat the seeds? Circle the correct picture.

   b. Which of these cannot live in a **closed** space for a long time? Mark the correct answers with a ✔.

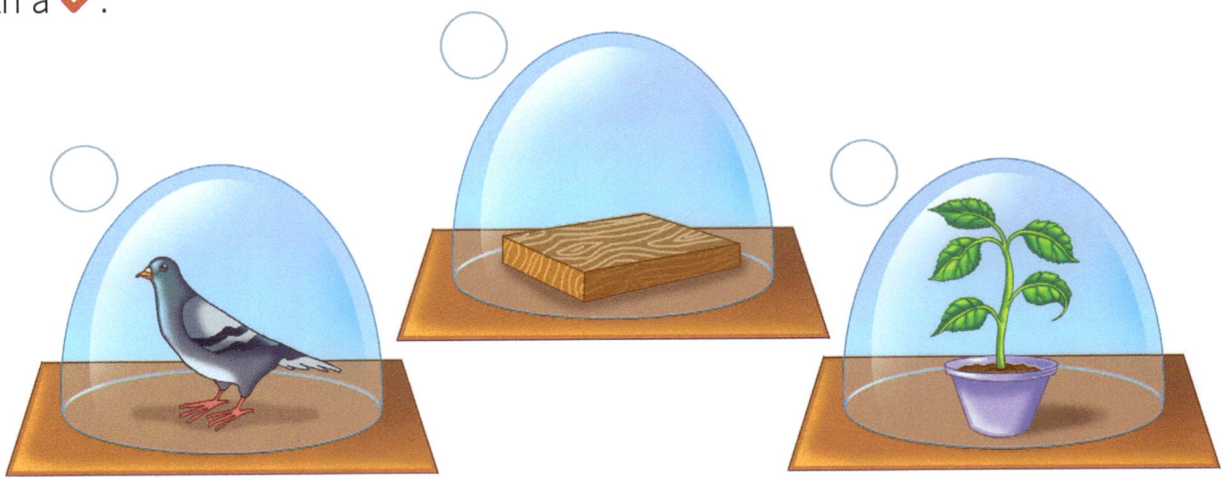

Scatter some bread crumbs in the park. What happens?

Just like you, animals and plants need **food**, **water** and **air** to live.

Word Focus

Crumbs are small pieces that fall from bread, cake or crackers.

Let's Practice

2. What does a rabbit need to live? Match. Relate

water

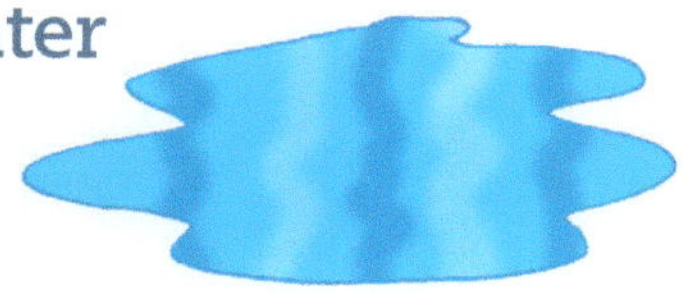

food

toy

air

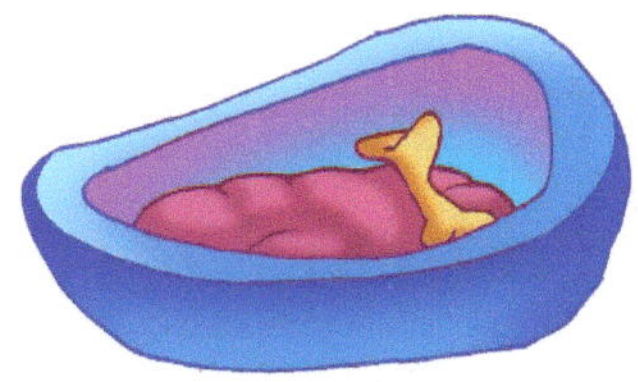

bed

Let's Summarize

Living things need **food**, **water** and **air** to survive.

Quiz Yourself

1. What makes a koala a **living thing**? Circle the correct answers.

It moves.

It grows.

It needs a bed.

It reproduces.

It drinks water.

It eats.

It breathes.

2. Why is a rock **not** a living thing?

Research Question

What Makes a Living Thing Alive?

What Do I Need?

- 3 jars with lids
- 3 bean seeds
- 3 bottle caps
- 3 small rocks
- water
- cotton
- notebook
- pencil

What Do I Do?

1. With the help of an adult, make small holes in the jar lids.
2. Cover the bottom of each jar with cotton.
3. Label one jar "Beans" and place the beans inside.
4. Label another jar "Bottle Caps" and place the bottle caps inside.
5. Label the last jar "Rocks" and place the rocks inside.
6. Add a little bit of water to each jar until the cotton is damp. Then put the lids on the jars.
7. Watch the jars for six days. Use a magnifying glass to observe.

Observing helps you get information about an object, a living thing or an event by using your **senses**. For example, you use your senses of **sight**, **smell**, **touch** and **hearing**. When you observe an object, you should study the color, shape, size and texture.

Results

1. What did you observe? Mark the correct answers with a ✔.

		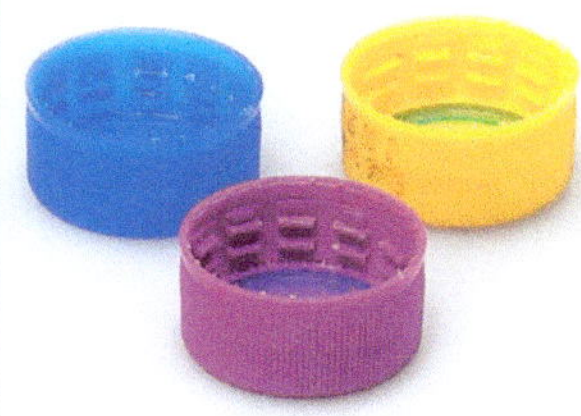	
Which grew after two days?			
Which grew after six days?			

Conclusion

1. Mark the living things with a ✔.

☐ bean sprouts ☐ bottle caps ☐ rocks

During this experiment, you used your sense of **sight** to understand which of the objects are living things. While **observing** the objects, you realized the beans **grew**.

2. Discuss with your classmates.

a. Why are the bean sprouts **living things**?

b. Why are the bottle caps and rocks **nonliving things**?

c. What **characteristics** of living things did you **observe**?

Domestic and Wild Animals

Let's Connect

1. Look at the picture. Mark the correct answers with a ✔. Recognize

		yes	no
a.	Can you have a dragonfly as a **pet**?		
b.	Do dragonflies need to be taken care of?		
c.	Do you need to **feed** your pets?		

Domestic animals live with people. People **feed** and **care** for them. Animals like dogs and horses are our friends and help us with certain activities. Dragonflies and tigers are **wild animals** that live in natural environments. They hunt for food or eat plants.

Education through Values

Your pet needs you! Take care of it, feed it, protect it and give it affection. Never hurt any living thing.

Challenge

Name two more domestic animals and two more wild animals.

Let's Practice

2. Put the puzzle together. Go to **Cutout 2** on **page 143**. Glue the puzzle pieces in the box. Identify

a. What kind of **animal** is it? Mark the answer with a ✓.

◯ domestic ◯ wild

b. Why did you choose that answer?

3. Make a collage of "Wild and Domestic Animals." Follow these instructions. Classify

- You will need a piece of paper, scissors, magazines and glue.
- Write the title at the top.
- Divide the paper in half with a line. On the left side write **Domestic Animals**. On the right side write **Wild Animals**.
- Find pictures of different animals in magazines. Cut them out and glue them on the correct side.

Let's Summarize

Domestic animals are our friends and helpers. In return, people **feed** and **take care of** them. **Wild animals** live in nature and feed themselves.

Animal Habitats

Let's Connect

1. Listen to the text that your teacher reads. Identify

There are animals that live and move on **land**. Other animals can only live in **water**.

There are some animals that live on **land** but move through the **air**.

Other animals live on **land** and in **water**.

a. How many different types of **environments** did you hear? ☐

b. Go to **Sticker Set 2** on **page 155**. Match the living things with their **environments**.

land	water	air & land	water & land

Animals live in different environments called **habitats**. Animals like squirrels, which live and move on land, are called **terrestrial**. Animals like whales, which live only in water, are called **aquatic**. Animals like eagles live on land and move through the air. These animals are called **aerial-terrestrial**. Animals like seals live in water and on land. These animals are called **aquatic-terrestrial**.

Let's Practice

2. Look at the photographs. Mark the correct answers with a ✔. Compare and contrast

sheep

shark

a. Can you see their **habitats**?
- ◯ yes
- ◯ no

b. Which is the shark's **habitat**?
- ◯ land
- ◯ water

c. Can sheep live in a shark's **habitat**?
- ◯ yes
- ◯ no

Let's Summarize

Types of Habitats
- terrestrial
- aquatic
- aerial-terrestrial
- aquatic-terrestrial

How Animals Move

Let's Connect

1. Look at the photographs. Mark each circle with the correct color. Identify

- animals that **run**, **jump** or **walk**
- animals that **swim**
- animals that **fly**
- animals that **drag** their bodies

Animals move in different ways to **travel** from one place to another. They move in different ways because of their **body types**. Some animals can walk, run or jump. Others can drag their bodies or fly with their wings. In water, animals can swim with their fins.

Challenge

Name three animals that move in different ways.

Fun Fact!

Penguins are birds, but they cannot fly. Their wings are fins that allow them to swim!

Let's Practice

2. Look at the photographs. Mark the correct answers with a ✔.
Compare and contrast

a.	It has legs.			
b.	It has wings.			

c. Where does the frog live? Where does the deer live?

d. What makes the deer and the butterfly different?

Let's Summarize

Animals can walk, run, jump, drag their bodies, fly with their wings or swim with their fins.

Quiz Yourself

1. Look at the picture.

a. Circle the **domestic animals** in  and the **wild animals** in .

b. Color the fishes' **habitat**. Is it the same habitat as the cow's?

c. Circle the body parts that the bee uses to **move**. Then circle the body parts the cow uses to move. Are their body parts the same?

Section 4

Birth and Nourishment of Animals

The Different Ways Animals Are Born

Let's Connect

1. Look at the pictures and listen to the information. Mark the correct answers with a ✔

Compare and contrast

marine turtles	mice

incubation period – 60 days	gestation period – 20 days

a. How are marine turtles **born**?

☐ They hatch from eggs. ☐ They are born from their mother's womb.

b. How are mice **born**?

☐ They hatch from eggs. ☐ They are born from their mother's womb.

c. Which animal is **born** in less time?

☐  ☐ 

Some animals, like turtles, eagles and fish, develop inside an egg. These animals are called **oviparous**. Other animals, like mice, dogs and koalas, develop inside the **womb** of their mothers. These animals are born from another living thing. They are called **viviparous**.

Challenge

Are you viviparous or oviparous?

Let's Practice

2. Go to **Cutout 3** on **page 143**. Glue the animals in the correct box. Classify

oviparous	viviparous

Let's Summarize

Ways Animals Are Born

- oviparous (hatch from eggs)
- viviparous (born from a womb)

Animal Teeth

Let's Connect

1. You need: a **pencil**, a **ruler** and **clay**. Experiment

- Pick up the pencil and a piece of clay.
- Put the clay on the table. Push the pencil into it. What happens?

- Pick up the ruler and a piece of clay.
- Put the clay on the table. Push the ruler into it like in the photograph. What happens?

Circle the correct answers.

a. Which was easier to **push** into the **clay**?  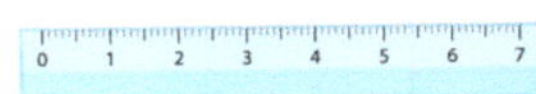

b. Which one looks like the **tooth** of a **puma**?  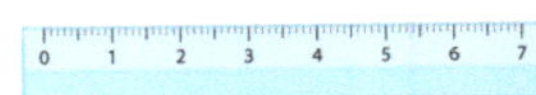

Animals that eat meat are called **carnivores**. Carnivores, like pumas and polar bears, have sharp teeth to tear into meat. Animals that eat plants, fruit and leaves are called **herbivores**. Herbivores, like sheep and cows, have big, flat teeth that allow them to grind up food. Animals that eat both meat and plants are called **omnivores**. Omnivores, like brown bears and foxes, have some sharp teeth and some flat teeth.

Fun Fact!

Birds can be carnivores, herbivores or omnivores. They don't have teeth; they use their beaks to break up food.

Let's Practice

2. Look at the photographs of the animals. Compare and contrast

a. How are they similar? Mark the correct answer with a ✔.

☐ diet ☐ teeth ☐ living things

b. How are they different? Mark the correct answer with a ✔.

☐ diet ☐ teeth ☐ living things

Word Focus

An animal's **diet** is what it eats.

Did you know that the dragonfly is a carnivore? It eats other bugs!

Let's Summarize

Animals can be **carnivores**, **herbivores** or **omnivores**.

Quiz Yourself

1. What are the **characteristics** of the animals in the pictures? Circle the correct answers.

a. How are they similar?

They are born from a womb.

They hatch from eggs.

b. How are they different?

Their diet is different.

They breathe differently.

Let's Check!

1. Circle the **living things** in and the **nonliving things** in .

ladybug

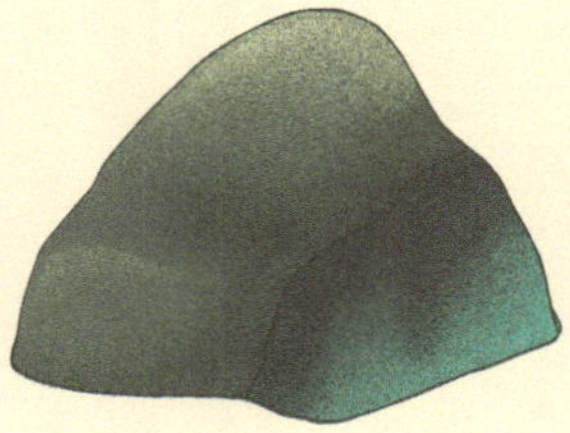
rock

flower

boy

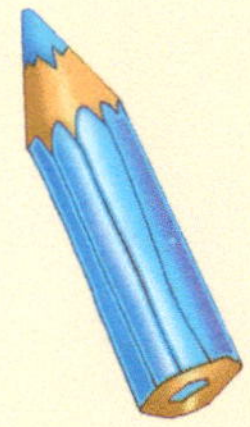
pencil

2. Match the pictures with the correct **characteristics** or **needs**.

hummingbird

eggs

zebra

1 year old

3 years old

reproduce

eat

grow

drink water

3. Write a **D** next to the domestic animals and a **W** next to the wild animal.

4. Look at the animals in the photographs. Color the correct answers.

a. Which of these is the fish's habitat?

- Air and land.
- Water.

b. How is a fish born?

- From an egg.
- From a womb.

c. Which part of its body does a dragonfly use to move?

- Wings.
- Fins.

d. What kind of animal is a dragonfly?

- A carnivore.
- An herbivore.

How Did You Do?

For each ☺ color a ⬭.

Section 5

Classifying Animals

Two or Four Legs

Let's Connect

1. Do you recognize the animals in the photographs? Differentiate

a. How many feet does the duck have? ☐

b. How many feet does the pig have? ☐

c. What do they use their feet for?

☐ to move ☐ to eat

d. How are they different?

In a terrestrial environment, animals move using their feet. Animals that walk on two feet, like ducks and ostriches, are called **bipeds**. Animals that walk on all four feet, like pigs and hippopotamuses, are called **quadrupeds**.

Did You Know...?

A duck has **webbed feet**.
A horse has **hooves**.
A dog has **paws**.

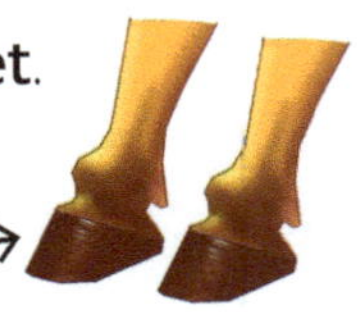

Education through Values

Some animals help people with disabilities. For example, a seeing-eye dog helps blind people do their daily activities.

Challenge

Name two more animals that are bipeds. Name two more animals that are quadrupeds.

Let's Practice

2. Go to **Cutout 4** on **page 145**. Glue the animals in the correct box. Classify

animals

biped	quadruped

3. Color the animals that move on four legs. Identify

Let's Summarize

Animals that are bipeds have two legs. Animals that are quadrupeds have four legs.

Big and Small

Let's Connect

1. Look at the pictures. Circle the correct answers. Compare and contrast

a. Are both animals dogs? yes no

b. Are they the same size? yes no

c. Can you see which is bigger? yes no

One characteristic of animals is their **size**. They can be big or small, depending on what they are compared to. Also, you can compare different kinds of animals. For example, you can compare a dog and a cat.

Did You Know...?

The blue whale is the biggest animal in the world. It can measure 34 meters long, or as long as eight cars in a row. The Philippine goldfish is one of the smallest animals. This goldfish is eight millimeters long. It is the same size as your fingernail!

Let's Practice

2. Look at the pictures.

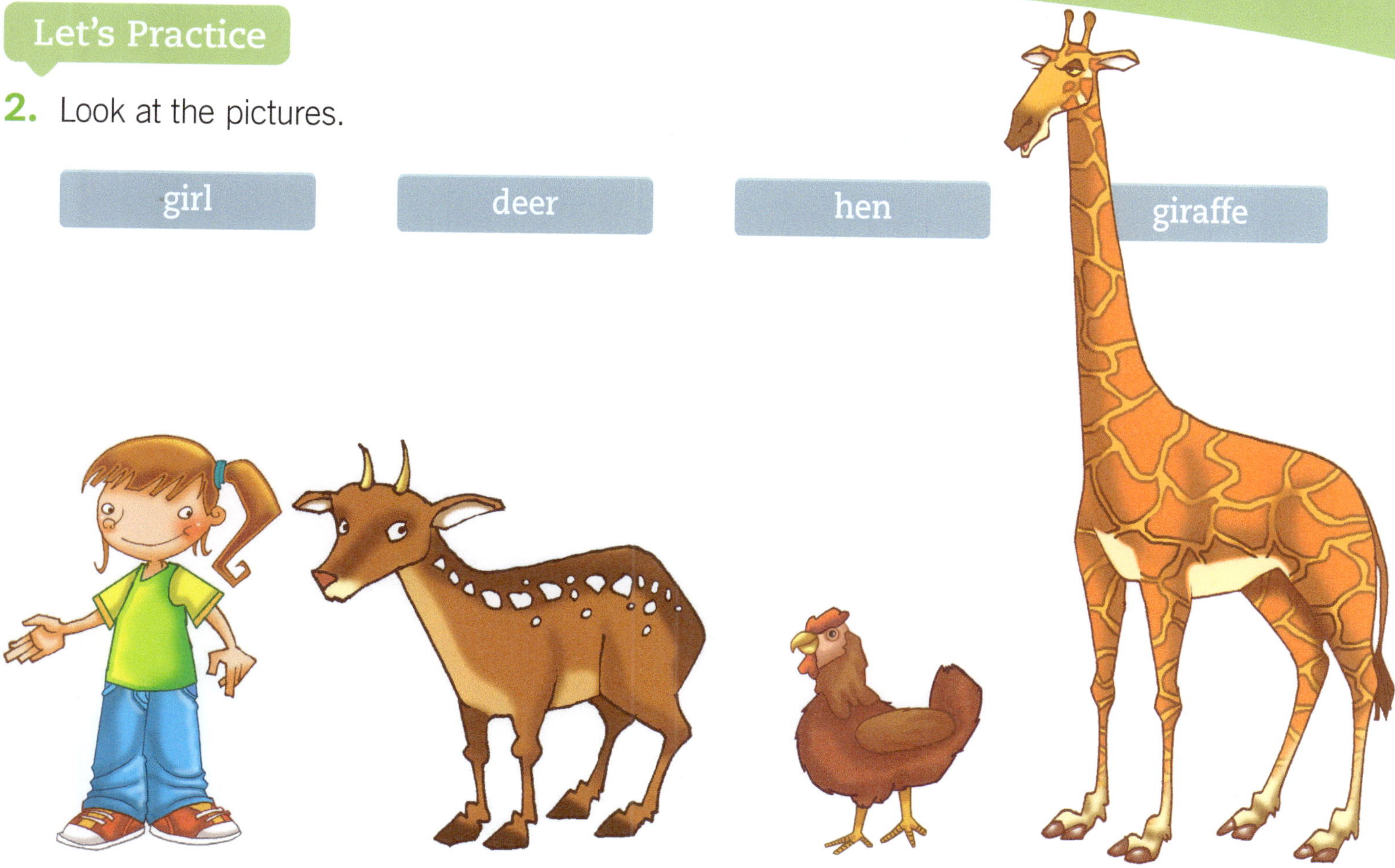

- Mark the circles with the correct color. Compare and contrast

bigger than the girl

smaller than the girl

a. The hen is ◯.

b. The giraffe is ◯.

Which animal is the most **similar** to the girl in size?

The deer.

Let's Summarize

Size is one characteristic of animals.

Word Focus

Similar is the opposite of different.

Different Body Coverings

Let's Connect

1. For this activity you need a **glass filled with ice** and a **sweater**. Experiment

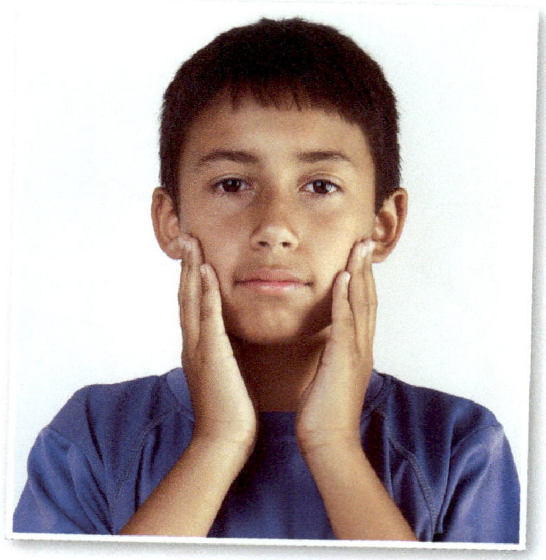

Hold the glass of ice in your hands and count to ten. Then put your hands on your face. How do they feel? Cold or warm?

Put your hands inside the sweater for a little while.

Now put your hands on your face. Do they feel the same or different?

a. What happened in each situation?

b. How is the sweater used in this experiment?

c. How do animals protect themselves from the cold?

Animals have different **body coverings**. Birds, like hummingbirds, have **feathers**. Mammals, like horses, have **hair** or **fur**. Fish and reptiles, like salmon and lizards, have **scales**. Body coverings protect animals from cold and heat. They prevent water loss and shelter animals from the environment. Body coverings do many other things, too.

Did You Know...?

Some animals don't have a body covering! Toads, frogs and other amphibians don't have hair, scales, fur or feathers.

Let's Practice

2. Look at the animals in the photographs. Circle the correct answers. Compare and contrast

a. Do they have the same body covering? yes no

b. Do both their body coverings help them? yes no

c. How do the body coverings help? They protect them from heat and cold. They help them move.

Let's Summarize

Animal body coverings can be **feathers**, **hair**, **fur** or **scales**.

Fun Fact!

Hair is what humans and many animals have. **Fur** is thick hair that covers the whole body. Other mammals have fur.

Quiz Yourself

1. Look at the pictures.

a. How many **feet** does the bird have? ☐

b. Circle the **biggest** animal.

c. Go to **Sticker Set 3** on **page 155**. Stick on the animal body coverings. Are they the same? Mark with a ✔.

☐ yes ☐ no

Play with the memory cards for animal body coverings. You can find them on **Activity Card 1**.

Section 6

Different Types of Animals

Learning about Animal Diversity

Let's Connect

1. Make your album of **world animals**. Go to **Sticker Set 4** on **pages 155 and 157**. Stick the animals in the correct places. Identify

elephant	hummingbird	polar bear
penguin	dolphin	salmon
crocodile	frog	rattlesnake

There are a wide variety of animals in the world, including mammals (elephant, polar bear, dolphin), birds (hummingbird, penguin), reptiles (crocodile, rattlesnake), fish (salmon) and amphibians (frog).

Let's Practice

2. Mark the correct answer with a ✔. Compare and contrast

a. Which animal has hair?

b. Which animal eats meat?

c. Which animal is oviparous?

Let's Summarize

Animal Diversity

- mammals
- birds
- reptiles
- fish
- amphibians

Did You Know...?

Pigeons are not from the Americas. They came from Europe, just like horses.

Taking Care of Animals

Let's Connect

1. Mark the actions that protect animals with a ✔. Identify

Did You Know...?

Endangered animals need more protection than other animals because there are not many of them left on the planet.

Many animals are endangered because humans destroy and pollute their habitats. These animals need protection. For example, tigers, pandas and mountain gorillas are endangered. We should take care of the environment to protect these animals.

Education through Values

All wild animals have the right to live freely in their natural environments. Do not destroy or pollute their homes!

Let's Practice

2. Which actions help protect the swan's habitat? Mark the correct answers with a ✔. Associate

- ◯ Do not throw garbage in lakes.
- ◯ Bring bread to feed them.
- ◯ Do not pick the plants near the lake.

Let's Summarize

When we take care of the environment, we are also taking care of our animals.

Quiz Yourself

1. Look at the pictures and answer.

a. Mark the picture that shows endangered animals with a ✔.

b. Why are there **fewer** animals in the second picture?

c. How can we take care of endangered animals?

Tip

Sentence starters:

1b. There are fewer animals because...

1c. We can...

What Did You Learn?

Mark the correct answer with a ✔.

1. According to your characteristics, what are you?

A I am a living thing.

B I am a nonliving thing.

2. What is one characteristic of all living things?

A They swim.

B They breathe.

3. A horse on a farm needs to be taken care of. It is a:

A wild animal.

B domestic animal.

4. Circle in blue the animal's **habitat.** Circle in red the body parts it uses to move.

Final Evaluation

5. Circle the correct answers according to the characteristics of the Bengal tiger.

a. It **hatches from an egg** / **is born from its mother's womb.**

b. It is **a carnivore** / **an herbivore** .

c. It is a **biped** / **quadruped** .

d. Compared to a horse, it is **bigger** / **smaller** .

e. Its body covering is **hair** / **feathers** .

f. Is it an endangered animal? **yes** **no**

Scientific Skill: Observe

6. Look at what the girl is doing. How can this action help birds? Mark with a ✔. It provides:

◯ food.

◯ shelter.

How Did You Do?

For each ☺ color a ⬭.

Unit 2

Plants Are Living Things

Key Words

sunlight

pot

shape

size

react

In this unit you will learn to:

- identify the parts of a plant.
- understand the characteristics and needs of plants.
- classify plants by size and parts.
- compare plants and propose ways to protect them.
- experiment using observation.

What Do You Know?

Initial Evaluation

1. Circle the **plants** in the picture. **How many** are there? ☐

2. Why are plants **living things**? Mark the correct answers with a ✓.

☐ They need water. ☐ They grow. ☐ They need sleep.

3. Color the **fruit** in the tree.

Scientific Skills: Observe and experiment

4. What do plants need to grow? Investigate.

What Do I Need?

A small potted plant, water, a pencil, graph paper and scissors.

What Do I Do?

- Cut a long, rectangular piece of graph paper.
- Put the plant on the table. Place the paper next to the plant where the stem begins.
- Draw a line on the paper next to the top of the plant. How many squares does the stem measure? Color the squares.
- Leave the plant close to a window for seven days. Water it every two days.
- Use a new piece of paper with squares. Place it next to the plant. How many squares does the stem measure now? Color the squares.

Results

Glue the pieces of paper in your notebook as shown in the picture.

a. Did the plant **grow**?

b. What did the plant **need** to grow?

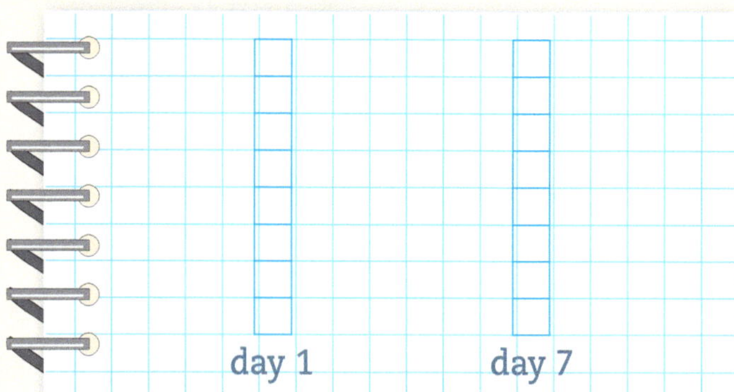

Parts of a Plant

Roots, Stem and Leaves

Let's Connect

1. With a classmate, choose a potted plant. Very carefully take the plant out of its pot. Observe its **parts**. Examine

2. Mark the **parts** of the **plant** you can see with a ✔. Identify

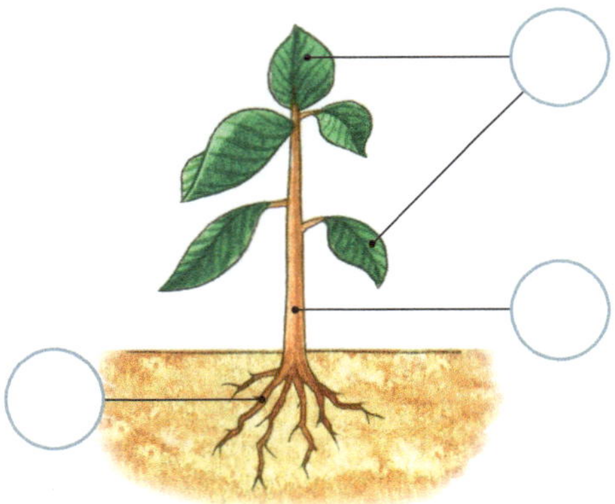

Word Focus

Leaves is the plural form of **leaf**.
Transport means to carry.

Plants have three basic parts.

- The **roots** grow underground. They **absorb** water and nutrients.
- The **stem** supports the plant. It also **transports** the water and nutrients.
- The **leaves** absorb sunlight and make food for the **plant**.

Let's Practice

3. Go to **Activity Card 2**. Identify

a. Cut out the parts of the plant and put them together.

b. Write the **name** of each part.

4. Draw the **missing parts**.

Education through Values

Sometimes in science, we use natural materials for experiments. Remember that it is very important to put things back in their natural environment. We need to be careful with plants and animals when we touch them.

Did You Know...?

A  is a 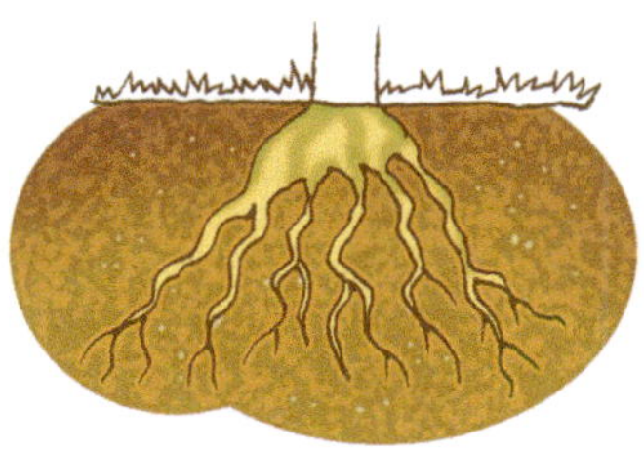, and 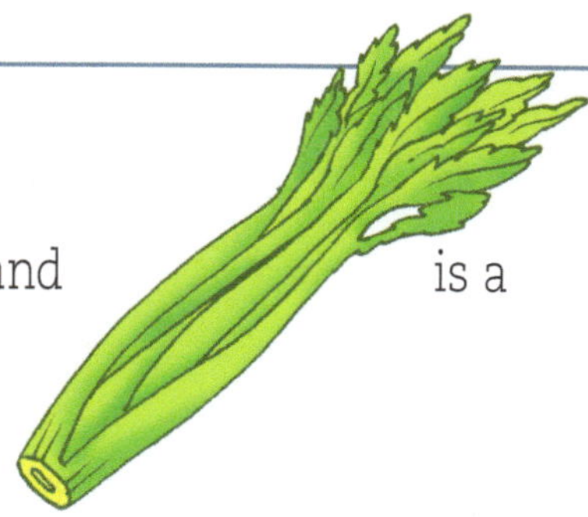 is a .

Let's Summarize

Plants have three basic parts: the roots, the stem and the leaves.

Parts of a Plant

Let's Connect

1. Color the flowers and the fruits. Identify

2. Mark where you think the seeds grow with a ✓. Infer

○ leaf ○ fruit ○ root

3. Find an apple, a pear or an orange. Your teacher will cut it in half. What is inside? Discover

Plants also have:

- **flowers** with different shapes, colors and scents. The flowers become fruits with seeds.
- **fruits** that protect the plant's seeds.
- **seeds** that make new plants.

Some plant parts are food, too. For example, artichokes and cauliflowers are flowers, grapes and pears are fruits, and lentils and peas are seeds.

Let's Practice

4. Color using the key. Identify

- fruit
- flower
- seed

peas

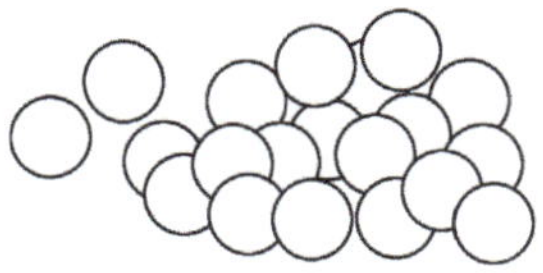

apple

pear

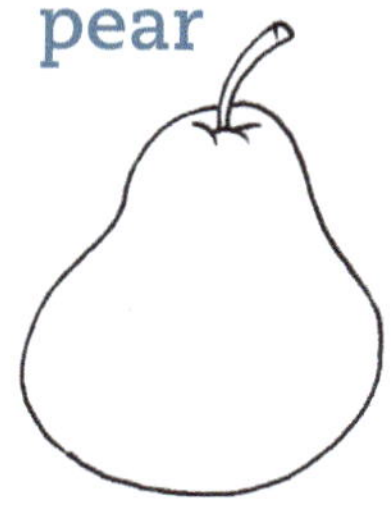

artichoke

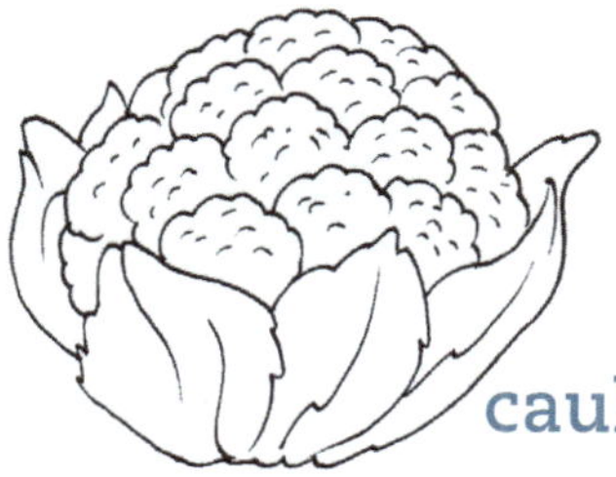

cauliflower

grapes

lentils

Let's Summarize

Plants can have flowers, fruits and seeds.

Quiz Yourself

1. Write the correct number in each box.

1. flower
2. fruit
3. leaf
4. stem
5. root
6. seed

Section
2 Plants

Characteristics of a Plant

Let's Connect

1. What do you see in the pictures? Interpret

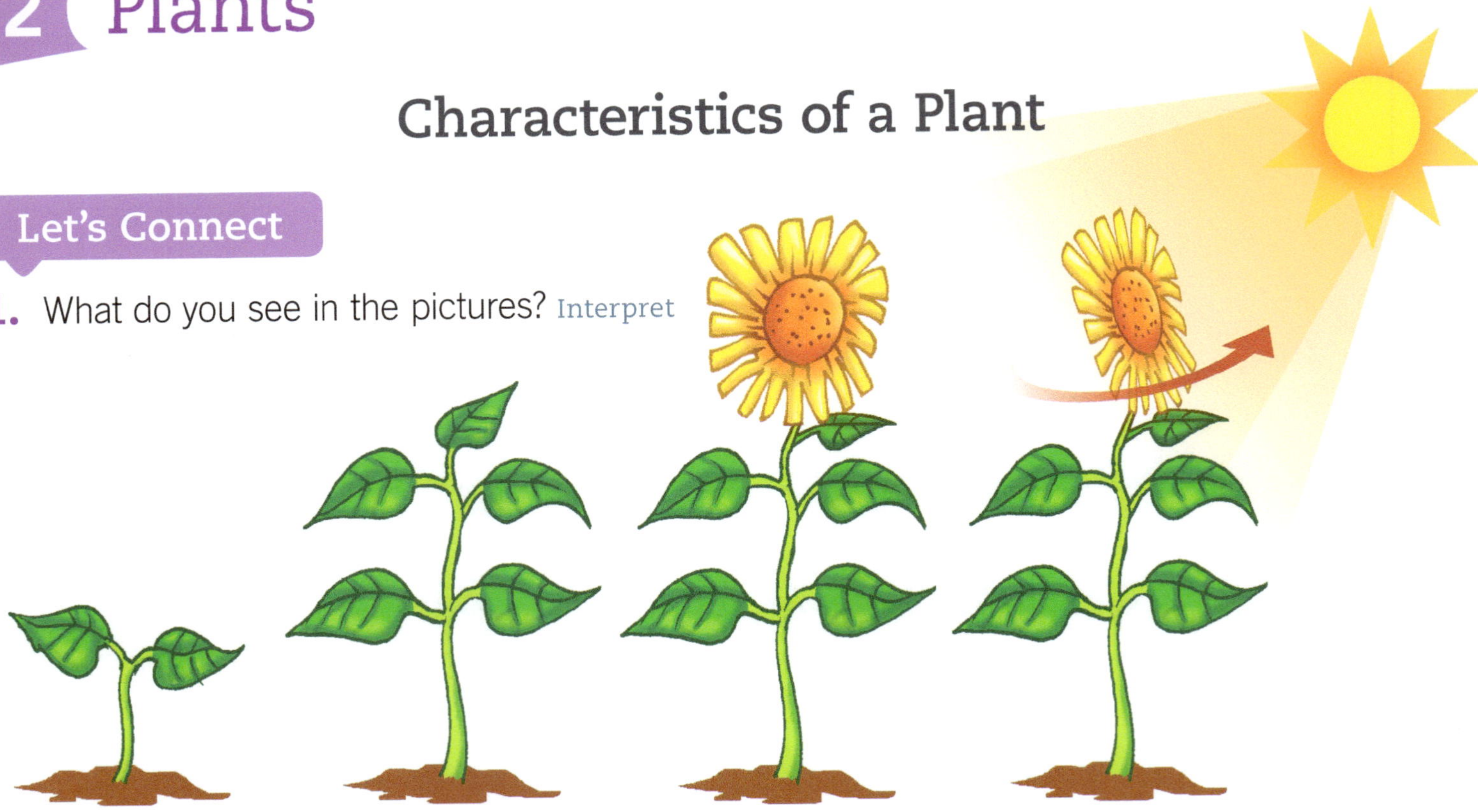

Mark the correct answers with a ✔.

a. ☐ plants **grow**

b. ☐ plants **react**

c. ☐ plants **move**

Look at the pictures again. Which shows that plants react? Discuss.

Did You Know...?

Plants react to different things. A sunflower moves toward the sun during the day. A mimosa closes its leaves when touched.

Plants, just like all living things, **grow**, **reproduce** and **react**. For example, they react to sunlight.

Let's Practice

2. Imagine you put a plant in a box with two holes, but **light only enters one hole**. In which direction will the **plant grow**? Draw a line in the direction you think the plant will grow. Predict

3. Do the **Science Lab** on **page 54** to check your prediction. Experiment

4. Think and answer. Look at the last picture in activity 1 again. Do you think the same thing will happen? Circle. Predict

yes no

Let's Summarize

Plants grow, reproduce and react.

What a Plant Needs

Let's Connect

1. Look at the pictures. Listen to what plants need to live. Identify

air

soil

sunlight

water

a. Mark the things that a plant needs to live and grow with a ✓.

sunlight

water

air

soil

Word Focus

Soil is another way to say dirt or earth. We plant seeds in soil and watch them grow!

What happens to a plant in a closed bag?

For plants to grow and live they need: **sunlight**, **water** and **air**. Most plants also need **soil**.

Did You Know...?

Sunlight is very important for plants. They use the light to make nutrients.

Let's Practice

2. Look at this plant. Color what it **needs**. Apply

○ sunlight

○ water

○ apples

○ soil

○ toys

○ air

Let's Summarize

To live, plants need sunlight, water and air. Most plants also need soil.

Quiz Yourself

1. Listen to your teacher and answer. Mark the correct answers with a ✔.

Anita went on vacation with her family. She left a plant in her room. The plant had no water or sunlight. It didn't grow and started to die.

a. Which **characteristic** of the plant is in the text?

○ growth ○ reproduction ○ reaction

b. What did the plant need to **live** and **grow** that it did not receive?

○ soil ○ sunlight ○ water ○ air

Science Lab

Research Question

In Which Direction Will the Plant Grow?

What Do I Need?

- a box (about 20 cm tall)
- a small potted plant
- a plastic cup
- scissors

photograph 1

What Do I Do?

1. Use the cup to draw a circle on each end of the box. Look at **photograph 1**.
2. With the help of an adult, cut out the circles.
3. Put the plant near a window.
4. Put the box on top of the plant. Look at **photograph 2**. The plant is in the middle, and one circle is facing the window.
5. Observe what happens each day for seven days.

photograph 2

As you know, when you **observe,** you use your senses, like sight, smell and touch, to get information about an object or event.
When you **experiment,** you are testing an event or change in a controlled way. **Experimenting** can help you find information to answer a **research question**.

Results

1. Complete the picture by drawing what you **observed** during the **experiment**.

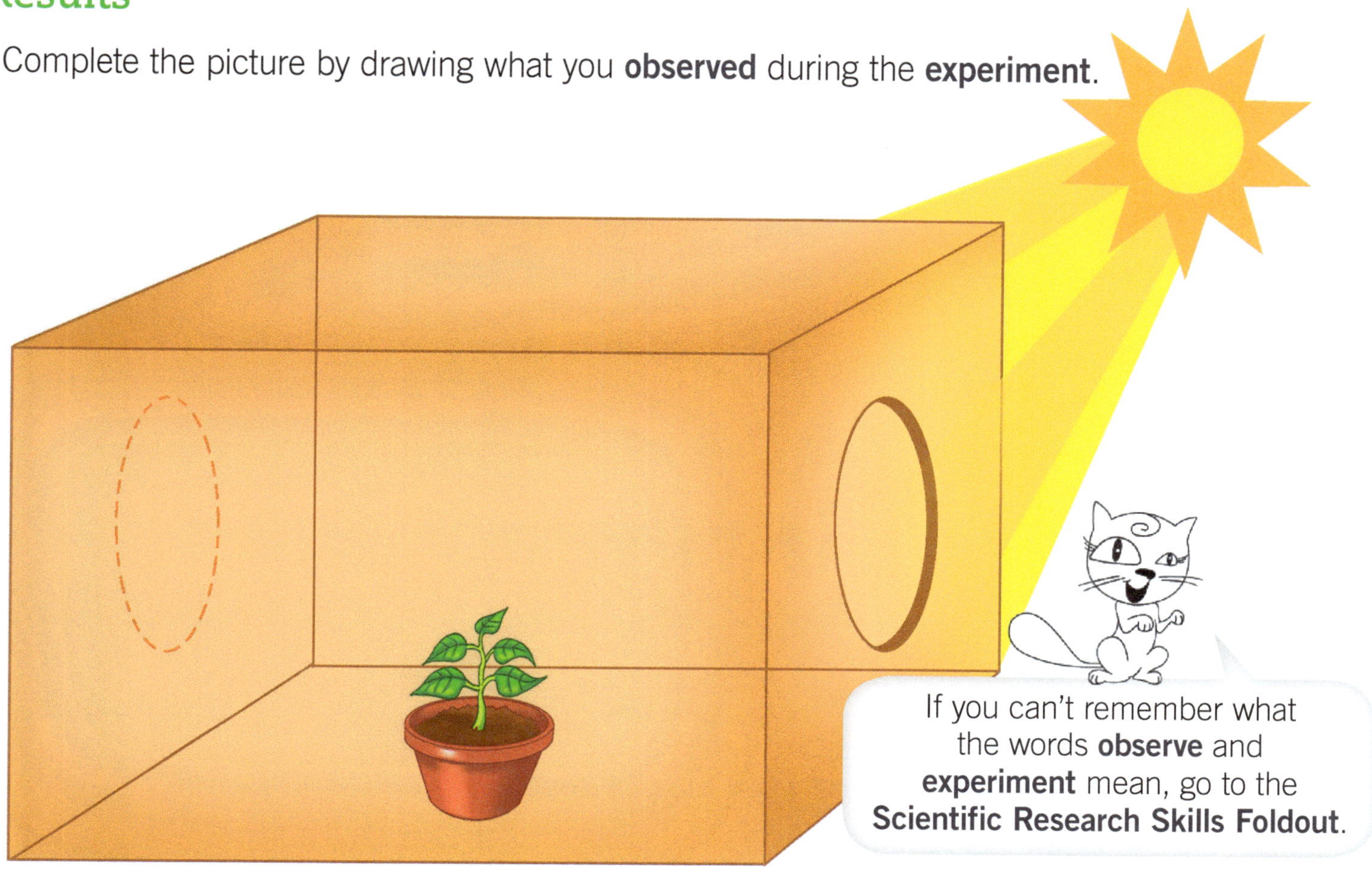

2. Go back to **page 51**. Is your drawing the same as your **prediction**? Circle.

yes　　　no

Conclusion

1. In which direction did the plant **grow**? Mark the correct answer with a ✓.

☐ **Toward** the sunlight.　　☐ **Away** from the sunlight.

2. Why did the plant grow in that direction? Mark the correct answer with a ✓.

☐ It needed water.　　☐ It needed sunlight.

3. In which **direction** did the plant grow? Discuss with your classmates.

Section 3

Classifying Plants

Big Plants and Small Plants

Let's Connect

1. For this activity you need to be in a place with **vegetation**. The playground, your backyard or a park are all suitable places. Discover

   a. Observe the **different** plants around you.

   b. Color the types of **plants** you see.

   c. What are the **differences** between the pictures?

   d. Are the plants **big** or **small**?

Plants can be different **sizes**.

Tree

Trees are **big** plants with thick stems called **trunks**.

Bush

Bushes are **smaller** plants with **branches** that grow from the ground.

Grass

Grasses are **small** plants with thin stems.

Let's Practice

2. Go to **Cutout 5** on **page 145**. Glue the plants in the correct boxes. Classify

Tree	Bush	Grass

Let's Summarize

Plants can be classified by size as trees, bushes or grasses.

Classifying Stems and Flowers

Let's Connect

1. Look at the photograph and circle the answer. Differentiate

a. Do the **stems** have the same **color** and **thickness**? yes no

b. Do you think both stems feel **soft**? yes no

Some **stems** are soft, thin and green. The stems of trees, called **trunks,** are rough, thick and brown.

c. Do the **flowers** have the same number of **petals**? yes no

d. Are all the **petals** the same **shape**? yes no

Flowers have petals. Some have many petals, while others have few. Some have **round** petals, and others have **long** ones. The colors vary, and many have petals of more than one color.

Let's Practice

2. Circle the **stems** (thin and green) in blue and the **trunks** (rough, thick and brown) in brown. Identify

3. Organize the petals in different ways on your desk. Classify
Think about how you could organize the petals on a chart.

What Do I Need?

- glue
- different flower petals

What Do I Do Next?

- Go to **Activity Card 3**. Glue the petals where they belong: **long** or **round**.

Education through Values

Respect nature by only using petals that are already on the ground.

Let's Summarize

Plants have flowers, stems and trunks. They are all different in size, color and shape.

Classifying Fruits and Seeds

Let's Connect

1. Look at the tables. Do the activity. Interpret

Fruit	
dry	fleshy

Seeds	
long	round

a. Match each description with the correct fruit.

- dry fruit
- fleshy fruit
- long seeds
- round seeds

The inside of a fruit can be **fleshy**, as in a banana or an apple. It can also be **dry**, as in an almond or a walnut.
Seeds can be **round**, like peas and lentils, or **long**, like sunflower seeds or pine nuts.

Let's Practice

2. Classifying fruits and seeds. Classify

What Do I Need?

- a big piece of construction paper
- glue
- scissors
- colored pencils

Classifying	
fruit	seeds

What Do I Do?

- Draw the table above on the construction paper.
- Go to **Cutout 6** on **page 147**. Glue the fruits and seeds in the correct area.

Let's Summarize

Fruits can be fleshy or dry.

Seeds can be round or long.

Quiz Yourself

1. Make groups using the key.

- bushes
- trunks
- long petals
- fleshy fruits
- round seeds

Let's Check!

1. Identify the **parts** of the **plant**. Color the plant using the key.

- fruit
- flower
- leaves
- stem
- roots
- seeds

2. Mark the **plant characteristics** with a ✔.

- ☐ growth
- ☐ reaction
- ☐ movement
- ☐ reproduction

3. What do plants need? Circle.

air

water

sunlight

scissors

rocks

soil

4. Order the **plants** by putting the **numbers** in the correct charts.

Stem or Trunk	
soft	rough

Fruits	
dry	fleshy

Seeds	
long	round

Size		
tree	bush	grass

Flowers	
many petals	few petals

How Did You Do?

For each ☺ color a ⬭.

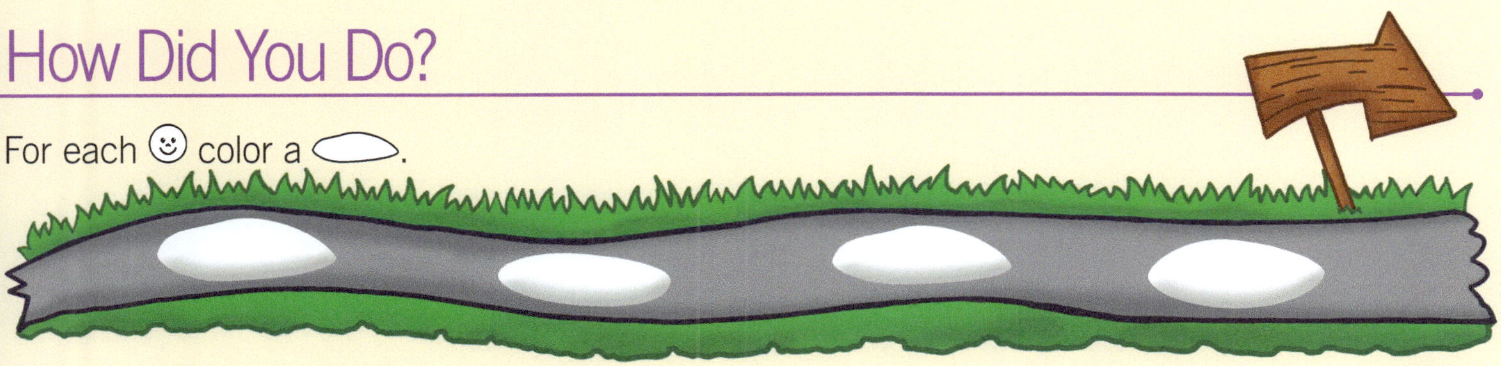

Section

4 Different Types of Plants

Learning about Plant Diversity

Let's Connect

1. Go to **Sticker Set 5** on **page 157**. Stick the plants in the correct boxes and trace their names. Recognize

giant redwood

olive

oak

fern

orange tree

cactus

wheat

palm

bamboo

There a lots of different plants in the world, including trees (giant redwood, olive, oak, orange tree, palm), bushes (fern) and grasses (wheat, bamboo).

Let's Practice

2. What are the **characteristics** of an orange tree? Color. Describe

◯ It is a tree.	◯ It is a bush.	◯ It has a rough trunk.
◯ It has fruit.	◯ It has seeds.	◯ It has flowers.

3. Compare the **plants**. Mark the correct boxes with a ✔. Compare

a. Which of the plants is a tree?		
b. Which plant has fruit?		

Discuss with your classmates.

c. How are they the **same**? How are they **different**?

Did You Know...?

Every country has a national plant. Some include the oak (Germany, UK, USA), the olive (Greece, Italy), the fern (New Zealand) and several types of palm trees (Saudi Arabia, Colombia, Cuba).

Let's Summarize

Some plants that grow in my country include the ________, the ________ and the ________.

Taking Care of Plants

Let's Connect

1. Mark the actions that protect plants with a ✔. Identify

Some actions, like planting trees, putting out campfires and walking on paths, help protect plants.

Education through Values

Recycling paper saves the lives of many trees!

Let's Practice

2. Which picture shows **protected** trees? Decide

Let's Summarize

Some actions, like planting trees and putting out campfires, help take care of plants.

Quiz Yourself

1. Look at the image and mark the correct answer with a ✔.

It has flowers.			
It has fruit.			
It is a tree.			
It has a thin trunk.			

2. How can you **protect** plants? Answer in your notebook.

What Did You Learn?

1. Complete the names of the three basic plant parts.

l _ _ f   s _ _ _ _   r _ _ _ _ s

2. Mark the correct answer with a ✔. Which is a **characteristic** of plants?

A They grow.

B They jump.

3. Color the pictures using the key.

stems or trunks   flowers   fruits   seeds

trees, bushes and grasses

4. Can many seeds grow in the same place? Make a **seedbed** to answer the question.

What Do I Need?

Cilantro seeds, a small pot, soil and water.

What Do I Do Next?

- Fill the pot halfway with soil.
- Place the seeds in the soil.
- Cover the seeds with soil, and water them.
- Leave the pot in a place that is good for plants to grow for 10 days.

a. What does this place need? Mark with a ✔.

☐ toys ☐ air

☐ soil ☐ sunlight

☐ a lightbulb ☐ water

b. What happened to the plants? Mark with a ✔.

☐ They grew. ☐ They did not grow.

c. Can many seeds grow in the same place? Discuss with your classmates.

How Did You Do?

For each ☺ color a ⬭.

Unit 3

The Five Senses and Your Health

Key Words

protect

loud

experiment

movement

communicate

In this unit you will learn to:

- identify the location and function of the senses of taste and smell and think of ways to protect them.
- identify the location and function of the senses of hearing, sight and touch and think of ways to protect them.
- describe healthy life habits.
- experiment with the sense of taste.

What Do You Know?

Initial Evaluation

1. Look at the picture. Circle the **body part** used for each activity.

- The boy **smells** the food.
- The baby **tastes** the food.
- The grandfather **reads** the newspaper.
- The girl **listens** to her father.
- The girl **touches** the baby.

2. Mark with a ✔ the foods that are on the table.

☐ vegetables ☐ cakes ☐ meat

Scientific Skill: Experiment

3. Do all objects feel the same when you touch them?

What Do I Need?

A scarf, a pencil and a pencil case.

What Do I Do?

- Close your eyes and touch the scarf.
- Repeat with the other objects.

Results

Mark your observations with a ✔.

	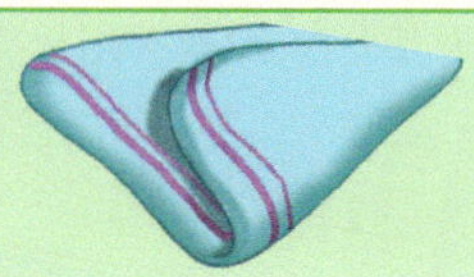	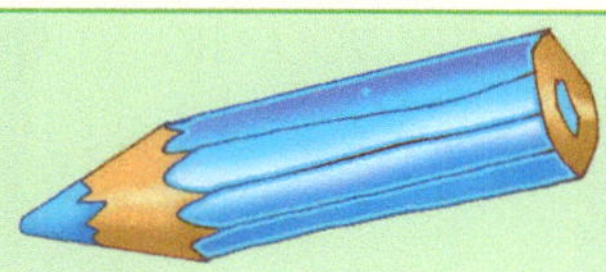	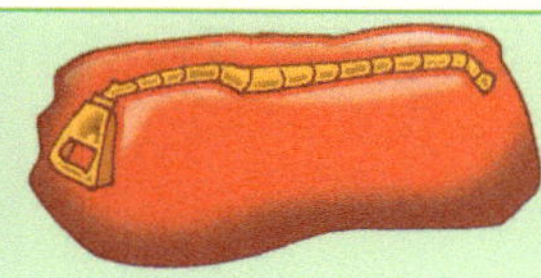
Hard			
Soft			
Smooth			
Rough			

a. Do all the objects **feel** the same? Discuss.

The Sense of Taste

Let's Connect

1. Circle the **body part** you use to **taste** a piece of fruit. Infer

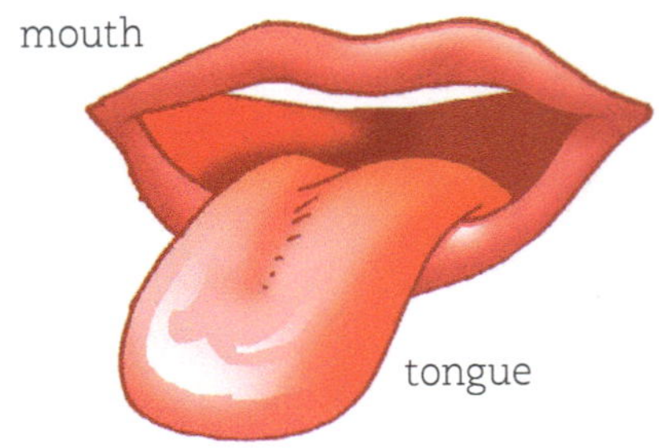

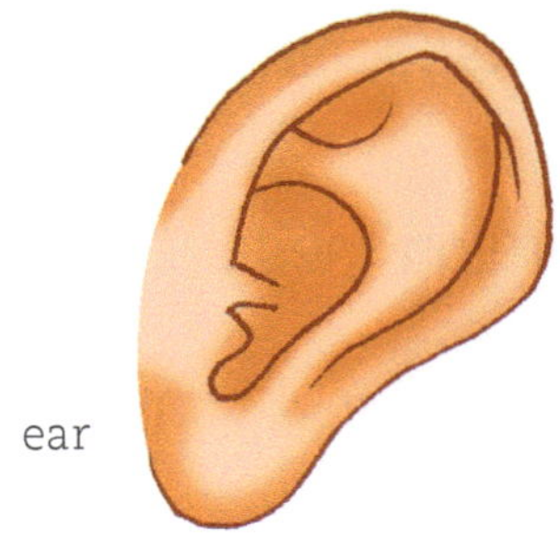

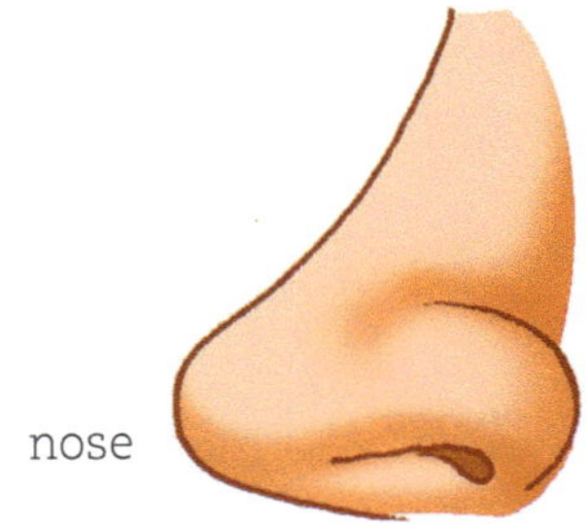

2. **Prove** your answer. Experiment

- Get an apple (or another fruit that you like), wash it and take a bite.
- Close your eyes. Which **body** part do you use to taste the fruit?
- Go to **Cutout 7** on **page 147**. Choose the body part you used to taste. Glue it in the box.

3. Did you get the same answer as you did in **question 1**? Mark with a ✔.

☐ yes ☐ no

4. Can you burn your tongue by eating hot foods?

☐ yes ☐ no

The sense of **taste** is related to the organ called the tongue, located in the mouth. Using your tongue you can taste sweet, salty, sour and bitter flavors. Be careful not to eat food that is too hot, or it will burn your tongue.

Let's Practice

5. Which foods are **sweet** and which are sour? Color using the key. Identify

sweet   sour

cantaloupe

orange

pickle

lemon

grapes

honey

6. Which word correctly completes the sentence? Describe

taste	smell

The tongue allows us to ______________________ different foods.

Did You Know...?

Babies taste with their tongues, palate and cheeks; butterflies taste with their feet; and worms taste with their entire bodies!

Let's Summarize

The sense of taste is related to the organ called the tongue, which allows us to taste different foods.

The Sense of Smell

Let's Connect

1. Think about how each of these things **smell**. Draw a ☺ if you like the smell. Draw a ☹ if you do not. Identify

fish

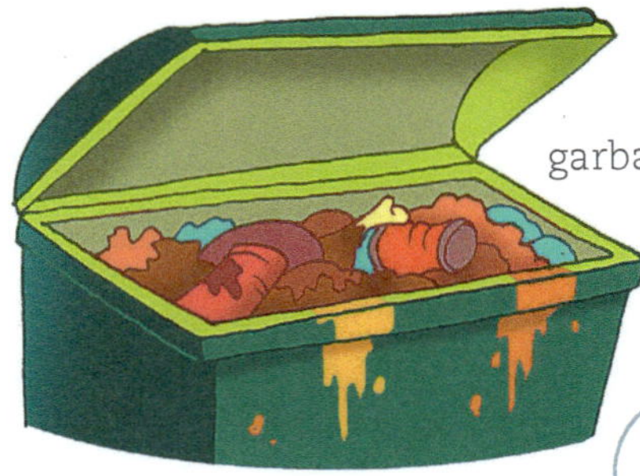

garbage

dumpster

flowers

watermelon

a. Which organ do you use to smell? Mark with a ✔.

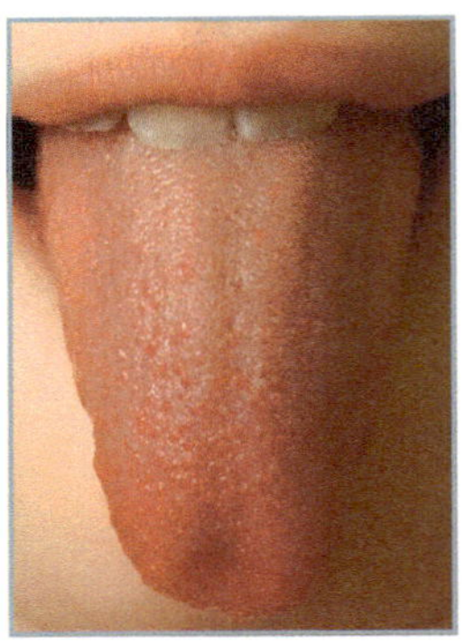

tongue

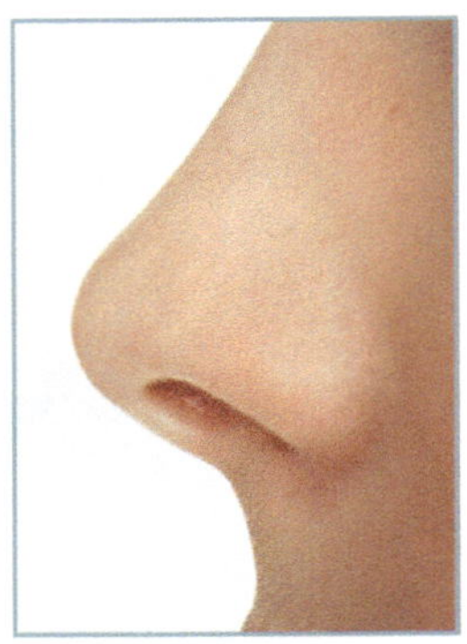

nose

The organ related to the sense of **smell** is the nose. You use your nose to smell nice smells, like flowers, and bad smells, like garbage. A smell can be good or bad depending on what you like. Take care of your nose by using tissues to blow it. **Never** use your fingers to pick your nose.

Let's Practice

2. Look at the picture. Use the words in the box to answer the questions.
Describe

steak
moldy
gross

Discuss.

a. Why do the **children** look **sick**?

b. Why does the **food smell bad**?

c. Which **organ** do you use to smell?

Let's Summarize

The sense of smell allows us to smell things using our nose.

Quiz Yourself

1. Match the **names of the senses** with the correct pictures. Answer the questions.

taste

smell

a. Which **organs** do we use to smell and taste? Where are they located?

b. What are the **functions** of these two senses?

c. How can you **take care** of these body parts? Name one way for each.

Section
2 Hearing, Sight and Touch

The Sense of Hearing

Let's Connect

1. Find a partner for the activity. Explore

- Collect these materials: a scarf, three pencils, scissors and a chair.
- Use the scarf to cover your partner's eyes.
- Use the objects to make various noises.
- The person who cannot see should **guess** which objects are being used.
- Mark the items your partner guessed correctly with a ✔.

		pencils	fingers	scissors	chair
			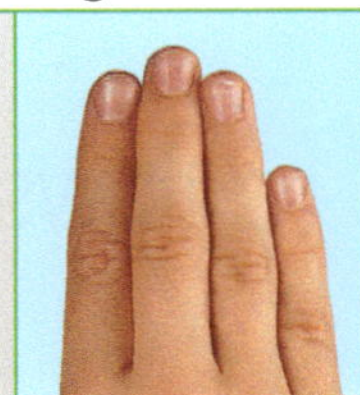	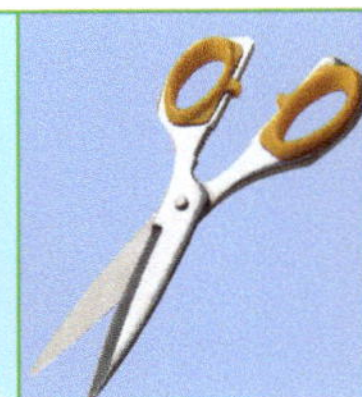	
a.	Make noise with your fingers				
b.	Hit the pencils together				
c.	Move the chair				
d.	Cut paper with the scissors				

2. Which **body part** allowed you to **hear** the sounds? Mark with a ✔. Identify

☐ tongue ☐ nose ☐ ears

We **hear** or **listen to** sounds with the help of the organs called the **ears**. The sense of **hearing** allows us to hear all the sounds around us, including loud **noises** we do not want to hear! **Protect** your ears by not listening to loud music and not yelling in the classroom.

Education through Values

Too much noise is called noise pollution. It makes the world a less peaceful place.
Be respectful of others, and do not make loud noises in public places.

Let's Practice

3. Look and the picture. Mark your answers with a ✔. Describe

a. Why are the children **covering their ears**?

☐ They are playing. ☐ There is too much noise.

b. Which **organ** do you use to hear sounds?

☐ nose ☐ ears

Discuss.

c. Why is it important not to make too much loud noise?

d. What can you do to not make **loud noises**?

Let's Summarize

The sense of hearing allows us to hear the sounds around us by using our ears.

Staying Healthy

Keep the volume low when you listen to music with headphones. This helps protect your sense of hearing.

Fun Fact!

Bats, dolphins, whales and other animals use their sense of hearing to "see." They send out sounds and listen to how the sounds have changed when they come back.

The Sense of Sight

Let's Connect

1. Find **six differences** between the pictures. Circle them in the picture on the right. Identify

a. Which **body part** helped you find the differences? Color.

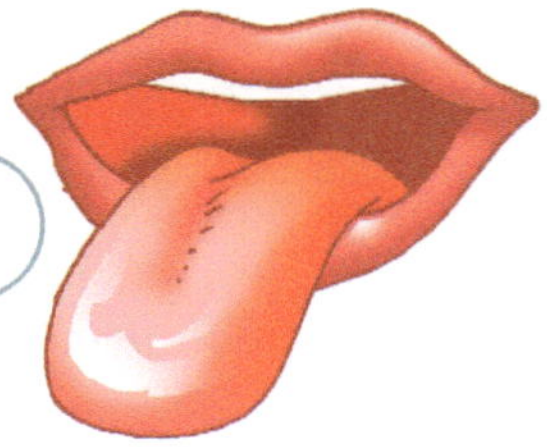

tongue

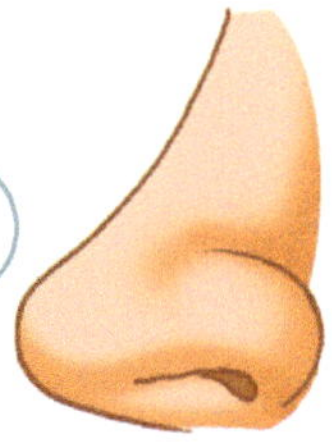

nose

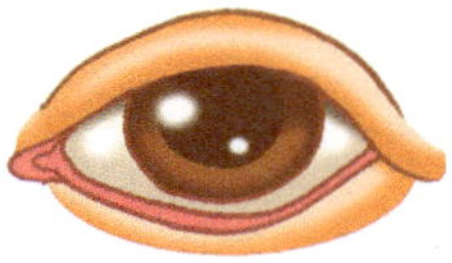

eye

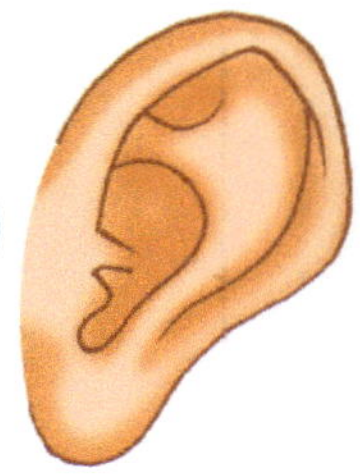

ear

Using the sense of **sight**, we can **see** everything around us with our **eyes**. We can see other living things, colors and objects. Protect your eyes by wearing sunglasses, not looking at bright lights and not rubbing them, especially with dirty hands.

Did You Know...?

Blind people (people who cannot see) use guide dogs (seeing-eye dogs) to help them move around and do their daily activities.

Let's Practice

2. Look at the pictures of the **sailboats**. Answer the questions.

a. Color the similarities in . Color the differences in .

☐ shape ☐ size ☐ color

b. Circle the **farthest** boat in and the **closest** boat in .

3. How does your sense of sight help you? Use the words to discuss the picture with a classmate. Describe

Let's Summarize

The sense of sight allows us to see everything around us with our eyes.

The Sense of Touch

Let's Connect

1. Look at the photographs and answer. Predict

a. How would your hands **feel** if you touched the **glass of ice**?

☐ cold

☐ hot

b. Can you pick up a cup of hot milk with your hands? Mark what would happen with a ✔.

The sense of **touch** allows you to feel contact with other people or things. Your **skin** is the organ that allows you to identify the characteristics of things, like whether they are hot or cold. You need to protect your skin from burns by not spending too much time in the sun and using sunblock.

Let's Practice

2. Which **organ** allows you to feel things? Color the correct part of the picture that represents you. Identify

3. Discuss. Describe

a. Is it correct to say we can **feel** with our whole **body**? Why?

b. What can you **feel** with your **sense of touch**?

Let's Summarize

The sense of touch allows you to feel things using your skin.

Did You Know...?

The skin is the largest organ of the body.

Quiz Yourself

1. Match each sense with the correct organ.

2. Discuss ways to protect each of the organs you have learned about.

Research Question

How Do Different Foods Taste?

What Do I Need?

- an orange
- a lemon
- chocolate
- an apple
- salted peanuts
- crackers
- a grapefruit
- olives
- water
- a plastic cup
- a place mat
- napkins

What Do I Do?

1. Place the foods on the place mat.
2. Taste the lemon. Then record your observations about its taste in the **Results** section.
3. Drink some water, and then try another food. Continue recording your observations in the table.
4. Taste all the foods. Remember to drink water after you try each one.

When you do an **experiment**, you are testing and examining an object or event. This will give you the information necessary to answer a **research question**.

Results

1. Mark your observations with a ✔.

	Salty	Sour	Sweet	Bitter
Lemon				
Orange				
Chocolate				
Apple				
Salted Peanuts				
Crackers				
Grapefruit				
Olives				

Conclusion

1. Go to **Sticker Set 6** on **page 159**. Stick the foods in the correct boxes.

Sour	Sweet	Salty	Bitter

2. Which of the five senses allows you to taste food? Mark with a ✔ and discuss.

☐ touch ☐ smell ☐ taste ☐ sight ☐ hearing

Let's Check!

1. Complete the crossword with the names of the **five senses**.

1. The sense you use to **listen** to music.
2. The sense related to your **nose**.
3. The sense related to your **tongue**.
4. The sense you use to **see** colors.
5. The sense you use to **feel** hot and cold.

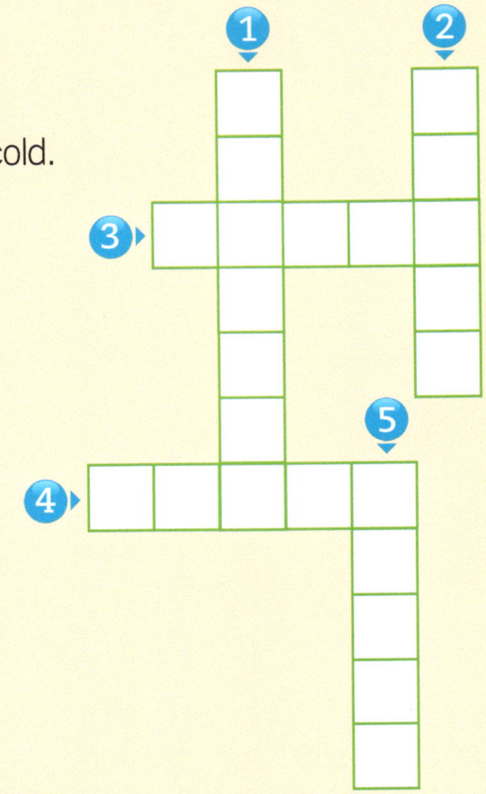

2. Look for the **organs** related to the **senses**. Color.

3. Complete the sentences.

a. I feel the texture of things using my sense of touch.

b. I smell perfume using my sense of smell.

c. I read a magazine using my sense of sight.

d. I listen to music using my sense of hearing.

e. I taste food using my sense of taste.

4. Draw a picture that shows the function of these **senses**.

smell	sight

How Did You Do?

For each ☺ color a ⬭.

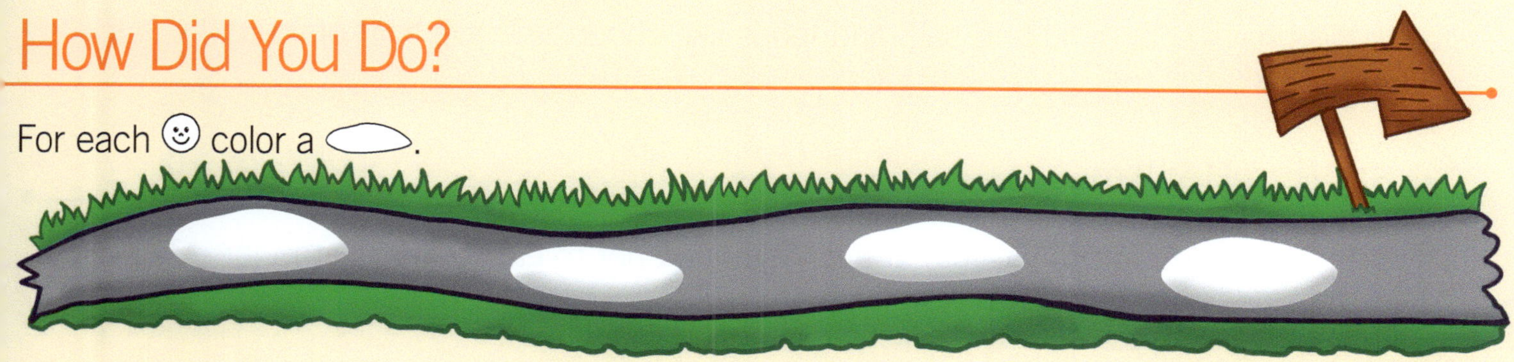

Healthy Foods

Let's Connect

1. What do you eat? Circle the foods you eat **daily**. Identify

celery

chicken

apple

candy

bananas

chocolate

lettuce

tomato

orange

cookies

a. Mark the foods you eat **the most** with a ✔.

- ☐ fruits and vegetables
- ☐ milk and meat
- ☐ french fries and candy
- ☐ cake and chocolate

Do not forget to drink enough water during the day!

To grow and be healthy, you need to eat a **balanced diet**. This means eating **healthy foods** in the right amounts.

You should eat fruits and vegetables, chicken, turkey, some red meat, cereals and dairy products. You should avoid **unhealthy foods** that are high in fat, salt or sugar. Foods like french fries have a lot of fat and salt, and foods like chocolate have a lot of fat and sugar.

Staying Healthy

It is very important to eat four times a day and not to eat very late at night. Also, avoid eating candy between meals!

Let's Practice

2. Make a healthy lunch. Describe

Go to **Cutout 8** on **page 149**. Glue foods on the plate to make a healthy lunch.

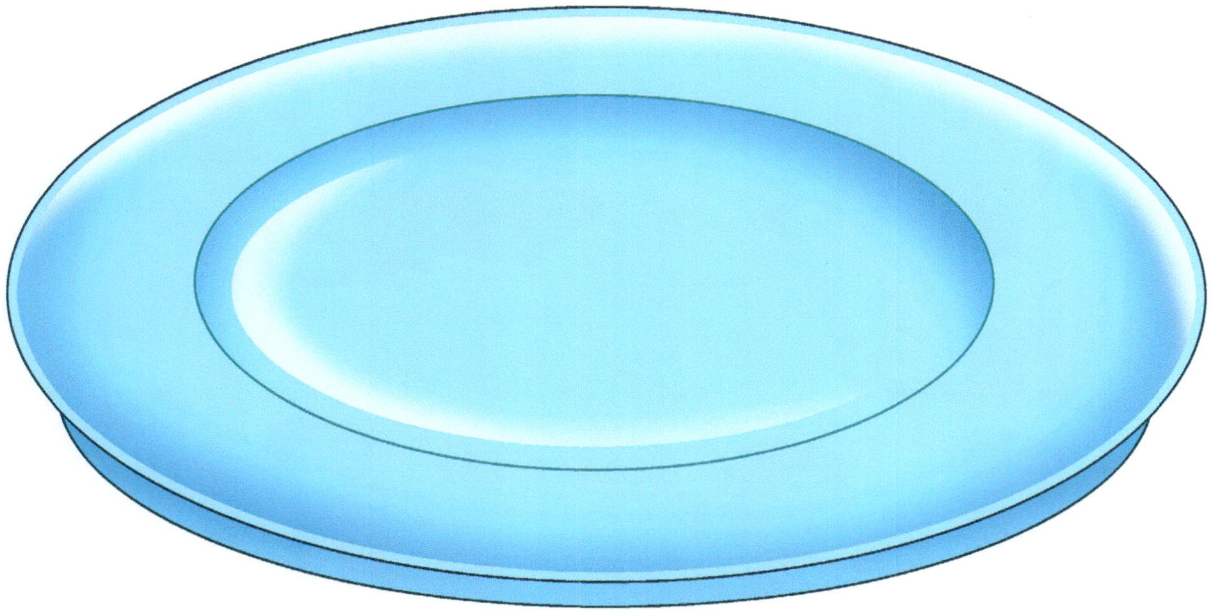

Challenge

Think of your favorite food or dish. Is it healthy or unhealthy? Discuss.

Discuss.

a. Why did you **choose** these foods?

b. Is your lunch the **same** as the others in class?

c. Why do we **wash** food before we eat it?

Did You Know...?

Obesity is a disease that has increased in many parts of the world over the last few years. Eat healthy food to avoid gaining weight or suffering from other diseases.

Let's Summarize

To grow and be healthy, it is necessary to eat a balanced diet.

Let's Exercise!

Let's Connect

1. Look at the pictures. Describe

use the computer

play video games

ride bicycles

play soccer

a. What is **happening** in each picture?

b. Color the circle next to your **favorite activity**.

c. What are the **differences** between the first two pictures and the second two pictures?

Exercise is all the **movements** you make during the day. Walking, cleaning the house, riding your bicycle and dancing are all forms of exercise, and they all keep you healthy.

Staying Healthy

Eating a balanced diet is only one part of being healthy. You also need to exercise and be active for at least an hour each day.

Let's Practice

2. Now that you know that **exercise keeps you healthy**, mark the activities you will do in the future with a ✔.

play basketball

play video games

walk

eat unhealthy food

Let's Summarize

Exercise is all the movements you make during the day that keep you healthy.

Good Hygiene

Let's Connect

1. Color using the key. Identify

good hygiene   change your habits

You wash fruits.

You do not wash your hands.

You do not wash your hair.

You take a shower.

You do not wash yourself.

You brush your teeth.

Discuss.

a. How should the children in the pictures that you marked **change**?

b. What do you do to stay **clean**?

c. Describe the pictures that show **good hygiene**.

Good hygiene means keeping your body clean by bathing, brushing your teeth, washing your hands and cutting your nails, among other things. These things will keep you healthy and prevent illnesses.

Education through Values

Why is good hygiene important?

Let's Practice

2. Discover the message using the secret code. Value

The message is:

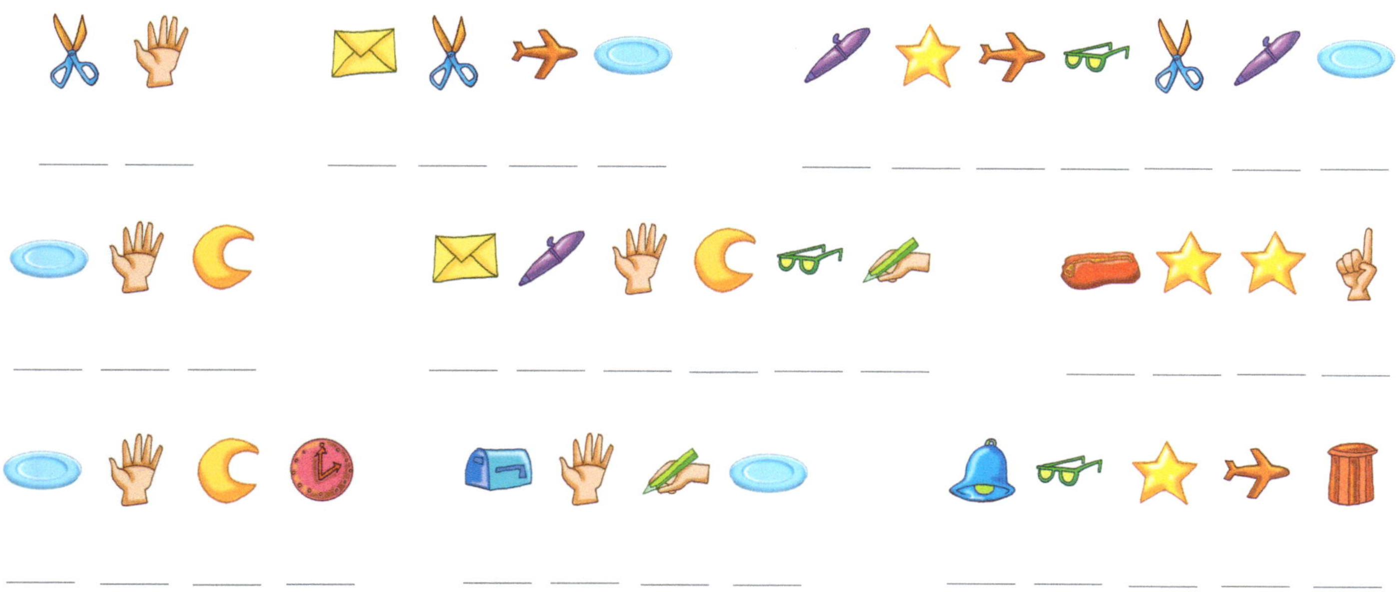

Let's Summarize

Good hygiene is one way to stay healthy and prevent illnesses.

Quiz Yourself

1. Go to **Activity Cards 4** and **5**. Play the game about healthy habits.

What Did You Learn?

1. Look at the pictures.

a. Write the number of each of the five senses in the correct circle.

1 sight **2** smell **3** touch **4** hearing **5** taste

b. Circle the sense organ used in each picture.

Final Evaluation

2. Go to **Activity Card 6**. Draw a ☺ or ☹ for the activities related to good or poor hygiene.

Scientific Skill: Experiment

3. Are potato chips healthy?

Products that are high in fat leave stains on paper. Prove it!

What Do I Need?

Potato chips, a piece of paper, a plastic plate and a kitchen towel.

What Do I Do?

- Spread the kitchen towel on the desk.
- Place the paper on top.
- Open the bag of potato chips and take out two.
- Drop them on the paper.
- Remove them and look at the paper.

Results

Mark the result with a ✔.

☐ The potato chips stained the paper.

☐ The potato chips did **not** stain the paper.

Are potato chips healthy? Discuss.

How Did You Do?

Find Test 3 Study Page

For each ☺ color a ⬭.

Materials and Their Properties

Key Words

change

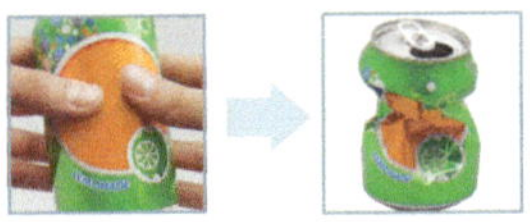

stretch

texture

recycle

reuse

In this unit you will learn to:

- describe different types of materials.
- classify materials by their properties and identify their uses.
- describe changes in materials caused by outside elements.
- design simple technological instruments.
- design and build an object using materials with appropriate properties.
- compare observations about the properties of materials.
- value the importance of reusing materials.

What Do You Know?

Initial Evaluation

1. Circle these **objects** in the picture.

pot

spoon

cup

jar

2. What **materials** are the objects made of? Use the words in the box.

metal - wood - plastic - glass

Scientific Skill: Compare observations

3. What will happen to ice and wood if they are heated?

What Do I Need?

Two plastic plates, ice, a piece of wood and a lamp.

What Do I Do?

- Put the ice on one plate and the wood on the other.
- Place the plates under the lamp for 20 minutes.

Results

a. What **happened** to the ice while it was under the lamp? Mark the correct answer with a ✓.

☐ It did not change. ☐ It melted.

b. Did the **same** thing happen to the wood? Mark with a ✓.

☐ yes ☐ no

c. Compare your results with your classmates' results. Are they the **same** or **different**?

Section 1
Types of Materials

Natural Materials

Let's Connect

1. Collect pieces of wood, wool yarn, cotton and leather. Touch each piece of material, **observe it**, and mark your observations with a ✔. Explore

	 wood	 wool	 cotton	 leather
It is soft.				
It is hard.				
It is rough.				
It is smooth.				

Which sense organs did you use?

2. If you were going to **build** a table, what **material** would you use? Color the box. Infer

☐ wood ☐ cotton ☐ leather

a. Explain why you chose this material.

b. Did your classmates choose the same material as you?

Objects are made from natural or artificial materials. **Natural materials** are found in nature. Cotton, cork and wood all come from plants, while leather and wool come from animals. Clay and copper both come from the ground.

Let's Practice

3. What can you make with these **natural materials**? Mark the correct answer with a ✔. Relate

wool yarn

sweater

chair

wood

table

T-shirt

4. Look at your pencil. Color the correct answers. Describe

a. What **material** is it made of? ☐ metal ☐ wood

b. Is it a **natural material**? ☐ yes ☐ no

Discuss.

c. What are the characteristics of **wood**?

d. Could you use only **metal** to make a pencil?

Can you make a cup from natural materials? Which ones?

Let's Summarize

Natural materials are found in nature.

Artificial Materials

Let's Connect

1. Circle the objects from activity 2 in the picture. Identify

2. What are the objects made of? Mark with a ✓. Identify

	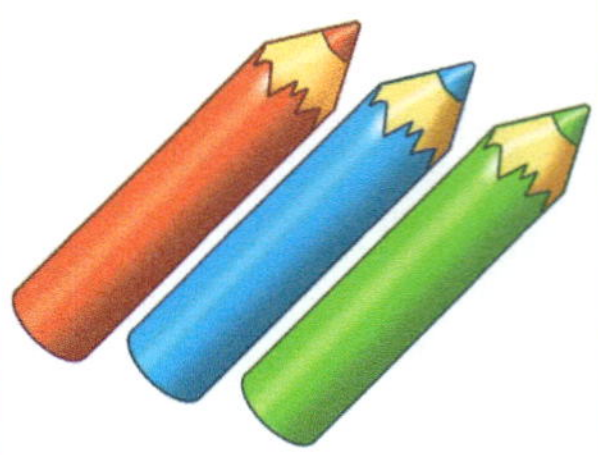			
Wood				
Glass				
Plastic				

Artificial materials are created by humans. Plastic, acrylic, glass, rubber and cement are all artificial.

Let's Practice

3. Look at the materials used to make an eraser and a pencil case. What are the **characteristics** of these materials? Answer the questions in your notebook. Describe

a. Are they made of **natural** or **artificial** materials?

b. Are the materials **hard** or **soft**?

c. Are the materials **fragile**? Could they **break** easily?

Education through Values

Some materials, like paper, glass and plastic, can be used to make new objects. Protect the environment by recycling!

Let's Summarize

Artificial materials are made by humans.

Quiz Yourself

1. Complete the information.

Object: ____________________

Material: ____________________

Natural or artificial: ____________________

Hard or soft: ____________________

Rough or smooth: ____________________

Hard or Soft?

Let's Connect

1. Look at the pictures and answer. Predict

a. Which material is easier to **scratch** using a paper clip? Mark with a ✓.

glass

chalk

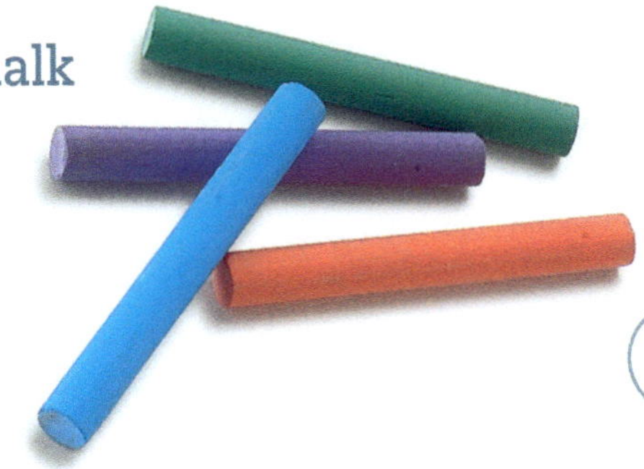

b. Which material can you use to draw? Mark with a ✓.

glass

chalk

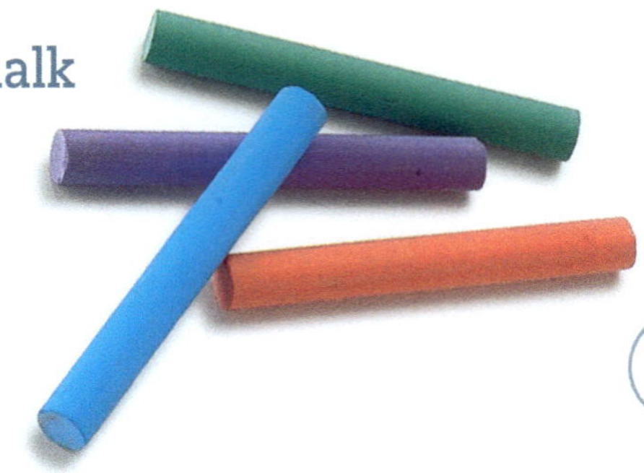

c. If the roof of a house were made of chalk, what would happen if it rained?

☐ The inside of the house would get wet.

☐ The inside of the house would **not** get wet.

To test what would happen, put a piece of chalk in water. Then take it out and compare it with dry chalk.

Soft materials, like chalk and clay, can be scratched easily. **Hard materials**, like glass or diamonds, are difficult to scratch. The practical uses of a material depend on the material's properties. You cannot use chalk for a roof!

Let's Practice

2. With a partner, collect these objects and materials: a paper clip, wood, clay, chalk, a pencil sharpener, a coin and metal scissors. Explore

- Pick up each one and scratch it with the paper clip.

a. Describe **what happened** to each material.

b. Which objects and materials could you scratch? Mark with a ✔.

☐ wood ☐ clay ☐ chalk

☐ pencil sharpener ☐ coin ☐ metal scissors

c. Put the materials in groups. Classify

soft	hard
______________________	______________________
______________________	______________________
______________________	______________________

3. Match each material with the correct object. Identify

rubber ○

metal ○

pot

mask

Let's Summarize

Materials can be hard or soft.

Stretchy or Flexible?

Let's Connect

This is called making observations.

1. Work in groups of three. Explore

- Collect a hair band and a hot water bottle.
- **Touch**, **bend**, **stretch** and **observe** the materials. Do they return to their original form afterward?

a. Mark the correct answers with a ✔.

	 hair band	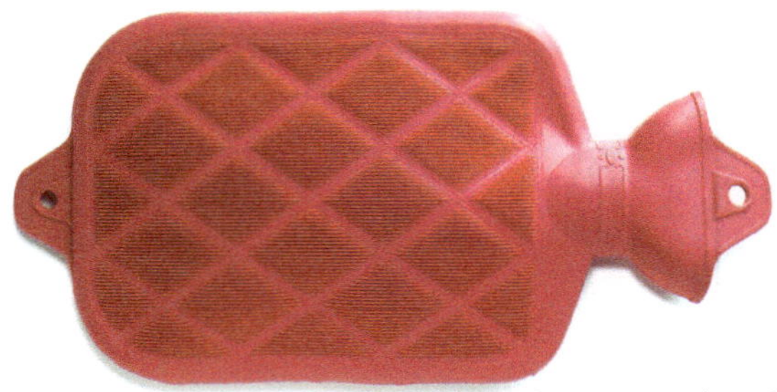 hot water bottle
Is it **hard**?		
Is it **soft**?		
Is it **stretchy**?		
Is it **flexible**?		

Materials that are **stretchy** change shape when you **pull** or **stretch** them, but they always return to their original shape. A **hair band** and a **hot water bottle** are stretchy. **Flexible** materials **bend** easily without breaking. For example, yarn is flexible, but glass and wood are not. All stretchy materials are flexible, but not all flexible materials are stretchy.

Did You Know...?

Some objects are made of materials that keep things warm. Styrofoam containers are used to store food but are bad for the environment.

What can you use instead of Styrofoam?

Let's Practice

2. Go to **Sticker Set 7** on **page 159**. Group the objects based on their properties. Classify

flexible

stretchy

3. What can you **make** with materials that have these **properties**? Color the correct answer. Associate

stretchy → ◯  ◯ 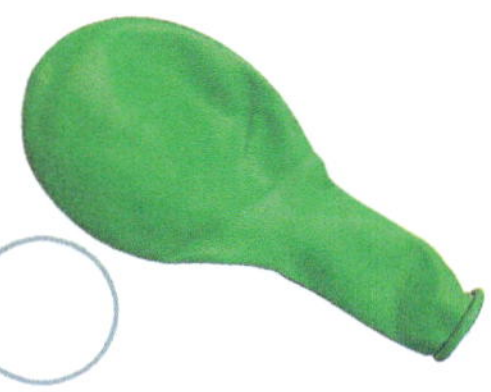

flexible → ◯  ◯ 

Challenge

Dancers and gymnasts are very flexible and always stretch before exercising. How are the flexibility and stretchiness of our bodies related to the concepts on this page? Teach two important stretches to your class.

Let's Summarize

Stretchy materials change shape when you pull them. Flexible materials bend easily without breaking.

Waterproof and Transparent

Let's Connect

1. Look at the picture. Color the correct answers. Infer

a. The boy is going to visit his grandfather. What should he **wear**?

☐ 

☐ 

b. Which material should be used to make an umbrella?

☐ wool

☐ plastic

Go to **Activity Card 7** and play dominos with the materials.

c. Does the material used to make the window allow the boy to **see** outside? Discuss.

Many objects are **waterproof**, meaning water cannot **pass through** them. Another property of materials is **transparency.** You can **see through transparent** materials, like glass or some types of plastic.

Let's Practice

2. Go to **Cutout 9** on **page 149**. Glue the objects in the correct boxes. Classify

waterproof materials	transparent materials

Let's Summarize

Waterproof materials do not allow water to pass through them. Transparent materials are see-through.

Quiz Yourself

1. What are the properties of these objects? Color using the key.

hard — waterproof — flexible

2. In your notebook, give an example of how we use each of these materials: copper, glass, rubber and transparent plastic.

Let's Check!

Mark the correct answers with a ✓.

1. What do wool and clay have **in common**?

A They are natural materials.

B They are artificial materials.

2. Which **material** comes from **trees**?

A Leather.

B Wood.

3. Mark the characteristics of each object with a ✓.

spoon

towel

Spoon:

- ☐ natural
- ☐ artificial
- ☐ soft
- ☐ hard
- ☐ smooth

Towel:

- ☐ natural
- ☐ artificial
- ☐ soft
- ☐ hard
- ☐ smooth

4. Write the numbers in the chart according to the materials' properties.

1 

3 

5 

2 

4 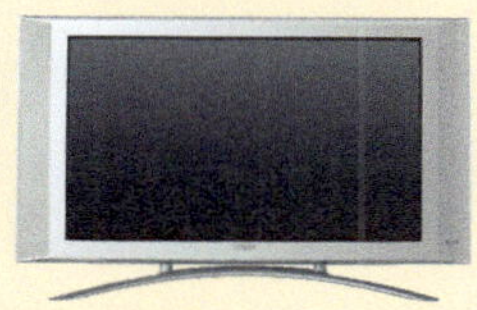

6 

Hard	Flexible	Waterproof

5. Match each **material** with the correct **property** and example of use.

elastic	transparent
rubber	stretchy
glass	flexible

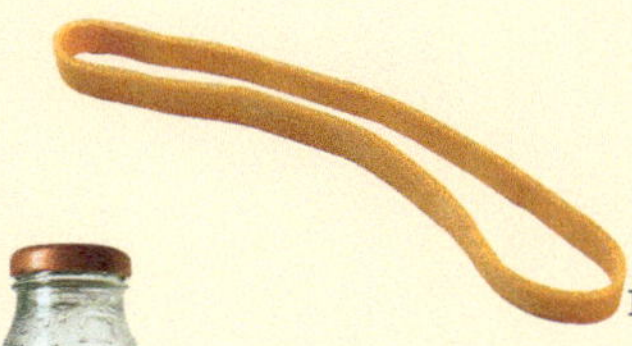

rubber band

bottle

tire

How Did You Do?

For each ☺ color a ⬭.

How Materials Change

How Applying Force Changes Materials

Let's Connect

1. Look at the pictures. Predict

a. What happens to an empty can if you squeeze it? Color.

○ 

○ 

b. What happens to an empty plastic bottle if you squeeze it? Mark the correct answer with a ✔.

○ 

○ 

c. How are these materials different? Discuss.

When you **squeeze** or **apply force** to some objects, their shape or size changes.

Let's Practice

2. For this activity you will need: a piece of clay, balloons, a metal spring and a piece of wood.

Explore

- Pick up the clay. **Stretch** it and **flatten** it.
- Do the same with the other objects.

a. Mark your observations with a ✔.

	It stretched.	It flattened.	It changed.	It did not change.
clay 				
balloons 				
metal spring 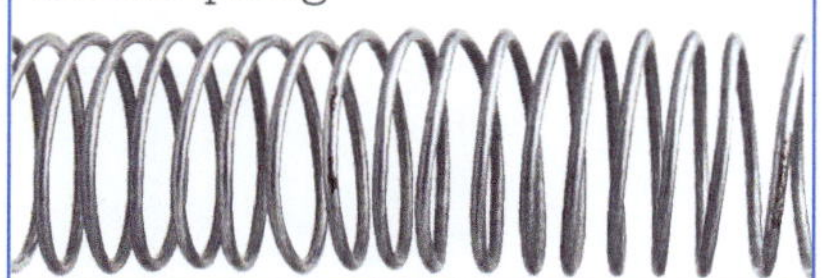				
wood 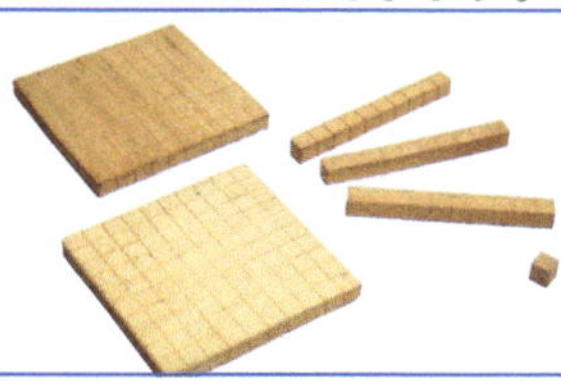				

b. What **changes** in the materials did you observe when you applied each type of force? Discuss.

c. What happened to the shape of each object?

Let's Summarize

Some materials change shape when you squeeze or stretch them.

How Light and Heat Change Materials

Let's Connect

1. Follow the instructions to complete the science experiment. Experiment

Collect two newspaper pages, two ice cubes and two transparent plastic cups.

- Put one ice cube in each cup. Put one cup in sunlight and the other in a freezer. Leave them there for two hours.
- Put one sheet of newspaper in sunlight and the other in **shade**. Leave them there for two days.

a. Did you **observe** any changes in the materials?

Ice: ☐ yes ☐ no

Newspaper: ☐ yes ☐ no

Word Focus

Shade means an area protected from the sun.

b. What happened to the ice when you put it in sunlight? Draw.

What happened to the ice you put in the freezer?

c. What happened to the newspaper? Mark with a ✔.

	In the Sunlight	In the Shade
It changed color.		
Its **texture** changed.		
Its size changed.		

Many materials change in shape, color, texture and size when they are exposed to **heat** or **light**. For example, the ice changed because of heat from the sun, and the newspaper changed because of light from the sun.

Let's Practice

2. What happens to the pen when it is exposed to heat? Look at the photographs and answer. Infer

a. Go to **Cutout 10** on **page 151**. Complete the sequence.

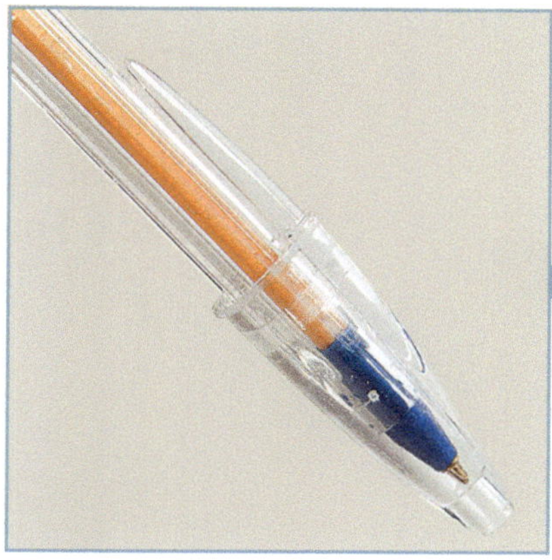

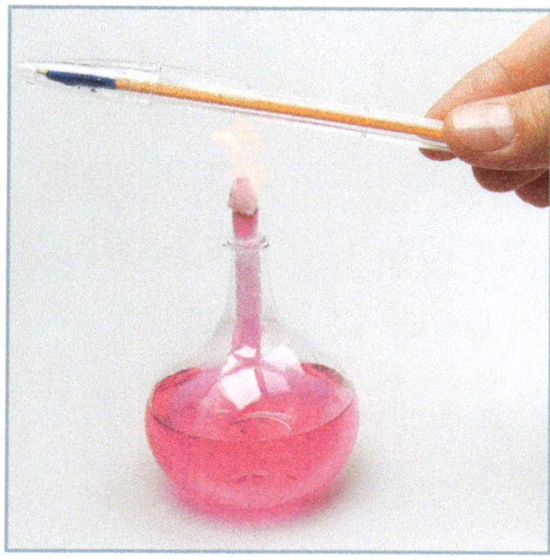

b. How did the pen **change**? Color.

☐ color ☐ size ☐ shape

c. Would the pen change the same way in the sun?

☐ yes ☐ no

d. How would the pen change if you left it in **water** for a long time?

☐ color ☐ size ☐ shape

Staying Healthy

Always be careful in the kitchen. The stove and the oven are both very hot when they are being used.

Fun Fact!

Clay is soft, but it becomes hard if you bake it. This is how pottery is made!

Let's Summarize

Some materials change in color, texture or size when exposed to heat or light.

How Water Changes Materials

Let's Connect

1. Collect two paper towels, a piece of paper, a plastic container, a spoon and water. Experiment

- Put one spoonful of water in the plastic container.
- Cover the water with a paper towel. Observe what happens.
- Then do the same with the piece of paper.

a. How did the paper towel change? Color.

b. How did the piece of paper change? Color.

c. Which type of paper would you use to dry a wet table? Discuss.

Some materials, when exposed to **water**, can change in shape, color or size. For example, paper towels can fall apart.

Education through Values

Plastic is waterproof, but it can also pollute the planet. Always remember to recycle!

Let's Practice

2. If you were to make a pot for a plant, what material would you use? Design

a. Mark the **material** you would use with a ✔.

☐ clay ☐ plastic ☐ paper ☐ Styrofoam

b. Which material would you not use? Mark with a ✔.

☐ clay ☐ plastic ☐ paper ☐ Styrofoam

c. What **shape** should the pot be? Discuss.

Let's Summarize

Some materials, when exposed to water, can change in shape, color or size.

Quiz Yourself

1. Go to **Cutout 11** on **page 151**. Glue the correct pictures in the boxes.

What would happen if you lit a match?	What would happen if you put a piece of cotton in water?

Research Question

Can I Make a Toy?

What Do I Need?

- Draw what toy you plan to make.
- Mark with a ✔ the materials you will need.

☐ cardboard ☐ poster board ☐ cloth ☐ metal ☐ ice cream stick ☐ scissors

What Do I Do?

1. Draw the steps you will follow to make the toy.

Step 1	Step 2	Step 3

Results

1. Select two materials. Then observe and compare them. Mark your observations with a ✔.

Property	Material 1	Material 2
Hard or **soft**: it is difficult or easy to scratch		
Stretchy: it stretches and returns to its original shape		
Flexible: it bends without breaking		
Transparent: you can see through it		
Waterproof: water cannot pass through it		

2. Draw the finished toy.

Conclusion

1. Did your classmates use the **same** materials as you did? Mark the answer with a ✔.

☐ yes ☐ no

2. Work with a classmate. What materials did your classmate use to make his or her toy?

____

3. What **properties** of the materials helped you build your toy? Mark with a ✔.

☐ hard	☐ soft	☐ stretchy
☐ flexible	☐ transparent	☐ waterproof

4. Think about the materials you used to make your toy. Could you use the same materials to make a toy boat? Discuss with your classmates.

5. Have a toy fair to show all the toys your class made. Tell everyone about the materials you used and their properties. Then have a secret gift exchange with your classmates and your new toys.

What Did You Learn?

1. Color the natural material in blue and the artificial material in red.

☐ wood ☐ plastic

2. Match the objects with the materials used to make them.

wood cloth metal

3. What are the properties of these objects? Mark with a ✔.

	Stretchy	Transparent	Flexible	Waterproof
 glass jar				
 rain boots				

4. What would **happen** to cardboard and plastic if you left them in water?

What Do I Need?

Two transparent plastic cups, water, a piece of cardboard and a bottle cap.

What Do I Do?

- Fill the cups halfway with water.
- Put the cardboard in one cup and the plastic bottle cap in the other. Observe what happens.
- After five minutes, take out the materials and let them dry on the table.

Results

a. Which material **changed** when exposed to water? Color the correct answer.

☐ the cardboard ☐ the bottle cap

b. On a piece of paper, draw how each material looked after taking it out of the water.

c. Compare your results with a classmate's results. Are they the **same** or **different**?

d. If you were going to make a house for your pet, what material would you use?

______________________________.

Find Test 4 Study Page

How Did You Do?

For each ☺ color a ⬭.

Unit 5

Times of Day and Seasons of the Year

Key Words

sky

stars

awake

asleep

clothing

In this unit you will learn to:

- describe earth's daily cycle and recognize how it affects living things and the environment.
- communicate about seasonal changes and their effects on living things and the environment.
- communicate and compare observations.
- value a healthy lifestyle.

What Do You Know?

Initial Evaluation

1. Read the questions and circle the correct answers in the pictures.

a. Which animal is **awake** when there is no **sunlight**?

b. Which plant **moves** toward the sun?

c. In which picture are the children **asleep**?

2. **Where** are the **sun** and the **moon** located? Go to **Sticker Set 8** on **page 159**. Glue the sun and the moon in the pictures.

Scientific Skill: Communicate

3. What do you see when there is sunlight and when there is no sunlight?

What Do I Need?

Graph paper and colored pencils.

What Do I Do?

- Choose a window in your house. Look outside when there is sunlight and when there is no sunlight and observe what you can see.

Results

Make two lists on the graph paper of things you see when there is sunlight and things you see when there is not. Are they the **same** or **different**?

Discuss your results

Go to **Activity Card 8**. Draw or make a collage of what you observed. Compare your drawings with your classmates' drawings.

Section 1
Earth's Daily Cycle

Day and Night

Let's Connect

1. Is it daytime everywhere on the planet at the same time? Do the activity with a classmate. Identify

- Collect a flashlight, a Styrofoam sphere and a marker.
- Draw an X on the sphere with the marker. The sphere will represent the planet, and the X will represent the location of your house.
- One of you holds the sphere with the X facing forward.
- Your partner shines the flashlight on the X.

a. Draw what you see.

Discuss.

b. If the light **represents** sunlight, is it day or night in your house?

There are 24 hours in a **day**. At the equator during the **daytime**, there are 12 hours of sunlight. Then during the **nighttime**, the sunlight shines in other places for 12 hours.

Did You Know...?

There are some places that have fewer hours of day and more of night. For example, in Alaska, the day lasts almost 24 hours during the summer.

Let's Practice

2. Look at the pictures and mark the correct answers with a ✔. Compare and contrast

- ◯ Living things are **asleep**.
- ◯ It is **daytime**.
- ◯ You can see **stars**.

- ◯ Living things are **asleep**.
- ◯ It is **daytime**.
- ◯ You can see **stars**.

a. What **activities** do you do during the **day**? What about at **night**? Discuss with your classmates.

Staying Healthy

Remember: you shouldn't spend too much time in the sun. When you do, use sunblock and a hat.

Does the night **sky** look the same when it is **cloudy**? Can you see the stars?

Let's Summarize

There are 24 hours in a day. When there is sunlight, we say it is daytime. When the sun goes down and is shining in other parts of the world, it is nighttime.

Times of Day

Let's Connect

1. Where in the sky is the sun **located** in each picture? Use the shadows to draw the sun in each picture. Predict

a. Discuss why you drew the sun in each location.

b. Try to observe your shadow at different times of day, like in the morning or at night.

A **day** can be divided into **four** different times: **morning**, **afternoon**, **evening** and **night**. Each time of day is different because of the location of the sun, and the presence of the moon and the stars in the sky. The times of day are also related to light and dark and heat or cold.

Education through Values

Take care of your body and always try to get enough sleep. If you go to bed early, you will wake up with more energy and your body will be healthier, too.

Let's Practice

2. With a partner, describe what you see in the pictures. Mark the correct answers with a ✔. Describe

a. Does the sun **shine** more **brightly** in the morning or in the evening?

☐ morning ☐ evening

b. When is it the **coldest**?

☐ afternoon ☐ night

Word Focus

Shine means to give off light.

Is the temperature the same in all parts of your country?

Let's Summarize

The times of day are different because of the location of the sun and the presence of the moon and stars, light or darkness and cold or heat.

Animals and Earth's Daily Cycle

Let's Connect

1. Go to **Cutout 12** on **page 153**. Glue the pictures in the correct boxes. Complete the activities. Recognize

day	night

a. Which animals are **active** during the **day**? Mark with a ✓.

☐ hens ☐ bats ☐ ducks ☐ owls

b. Which animals are **active** at **night**? Mark with a ✓.

☐ hens ☐ bats ☐ ducks ☐ owls

Animals that are awake and active during the day are called **diurnal** animals. Animals that are awake and active at night are called **nocturnal** animals.

Did You Know...?

Some nocturnal animals, like owls and cats, can see well at night. Others have special senses: aardvarks can smell and hear insects, and bats use sound to navigate and hunt.

Let's Practice

2. How are these animals **different**? Color the correct answer. Compare and contrast

- ◯ They are active during the day. ◯
- ◯ They have a great sense of sight. ◯

Let's Summarize

Animals that are active during the day are called diurnal. Those that are active at night are called nocturnal.

Quiz Yourself

1. Complete by drawing an activity for each empty box. Think about the characteristics of each **time of day**.

afternoon

night

Let's Check!

1. How are nighttime and daytime different? Circle in picture (1) the things that are different from nighttime.

(1)

(2)

2. Go to **Cutout 13** on **page 153**. Glue the pictures in the correct order.

3. Color in [red] what you normally do during the day. Color in [blue] what you do during the night.

4. Look at the photographs. Mark the correct answers with a ✓.

a. The hen **eats**:

☐ During the day. ☐ At night.

b. What helps the owl **eat** at **night**?

☐ Its sense of sight. ☐ Its sense of smell.

How Did You Do?

For each ☺ color a ⬭.

Section
2 The Four Seasons

Fall, Winter, Spring and Summer

Let's Connect

1. What do you think the tree looks like during each month? Draw your answers. Predict

a. How does the tree change? Discuss.

Every **year** has **four** seasons: fall or autumn, winter, spring and summer. Each season affects plants, animal behavior, temperature and the clothes we wear.

In which season does the sun go down the earliest?

Let's Practice

2. Read about each season. Match the descriptions with the pictures. Relate

- In the fall, leaves fall off the trees, the temperature lowers, and it becomes colder.
- In the winter, some trees have no leaves. It is the coldest season, and it snows in some places.
- In the spring, flowers bloom and the temperature rises.
- In the summer, we see fruits on trees, and the temperature is warmer than in the other seasons.

3. Look closely at the picture. Use the questions to help you describe the picture in your notebook. Describe

a. How does the tree **look**?

b. What are the children wearing? Describe the children's **clothing**.

c. What **season** is it?

d. Can birds make **nests** during this **season**?

Is it warm or cold when the **temperature** is low?

Let's Summarize

Every year has four seasons: fall or autumn, winter, spring and summer.

Living Things and the Seasons

Let's Connect

1. Look at the pictures and answer the questions. Infer

a. What do you see in each picture? Discuss.

b. Match the pictures with the seasons. Write the numbers in the correct boxes.

☐ fall ☐ winter ☐ spring ☐ summer

During the four seasons, living things and the environment change. In the fall, leaves fall from the trees and some animals **migrate**. In the winter, people wear warmer clothing and animals hibernate. In the spring, many animals reproduce and plants grow. Finally, in the summer, trees are full of fruits, the temperature is hot, and people wear less clothing.

Word Focus

A living thing **migrates** when it changes its location and climate to find food or reproduce.

Let's Practice

2. Look at the picture. Mark the correct answers with a ✔. Describe

a. What is the turtle doing?

☐ It is hibernating. ☐ It is looking for food.

b. What season is it?

☐ fall ☐ winter

Let's Summarize

During the four seasons, the environment changes.

Quiz Yourself

1. Go to **Activity Card 9** and draw the season in which you were born. You can also use cutouts from magazines or other sources to decorate your drawing.

Think about these questions:

a. How do the trees **look** during this season?

b. What **clothing** do you **wear**?

c. What **activities** can you do?

d. What is the weather like during this season?

Research Question

How Does Sunlight Affect Daily Activities?

What Do I Need?

- a notebook
- a pencil
- colored pencils
- an alcohol thermometer
- a clock

What Do I Do?

1. When you leave for school in the morning, write down the time and **observe** your surroundings. Look at the light, the trees and the plants. Observe what people are wearing, the location of the sun, and the temperature (hot, warm or cold). Write your observations in your notebook in boxes like the ones in the **Results** section below.

   Important: If you have an alcohol thermometer, you can measure the **exact** temperature with the help of an adult.

2. Repeat the same procedure at lunchtime, when you eat dinner and before you go to sleep. **Record** all your observations in the results boxes.

To record is to write down information from observations in a clear and organized way. You can present the information in pictures, tables or graphs.

Results

1. In your notebook, draw four boxes like the example below. This is where you will record your results.

Observation No. __

Time: ______________________________

Temperature: ______________________________

Observations: ______________________________

____

Conclusion

1. Draw your observations in each box. Then talk about or **communicate** your results.

To Communicate is to give information to others verbally, in writing or in another form.

morning	afternoon
Time:	Time:

evening	night
Time:	Time:

2. Compare your **conclusions** with your classmates' conclusions.
3. What **activities** do you do in the morning and in the afternoon?
4. How does sunlight affect our daily activities?

What Did You Learn?

1. Mark the correct answer with a ✔. What is the difference between day and night?

A During the day you go to school, and at night you play.

B During the day you see stars, and at night you see the moon.

C During the day it is light, and at night it is dark.

2. Look at the picture and do the activities.

a. Number: 1 morning, 2 afternoon, 3 evening and 4 night.

b. Circle the **diurnal animals** (active during the day) in red. Circle the **nocturnal animals** (active at night) in blue.

3. How do you know if a photograph was taken during the summer? Let's investigate!

Ben's teacher has asked him to bring in a photograph of himself when he was younger. The only requirement is that the photograph shows one of the four seasons. Ben wants to choose one that shows the summer. What characteristics should his photograph have?

What Do I Need?

White paper, a pencil, colored pencils and markers or paint.

What Do I Do?

- In your notebook, write a list of all the characteristics of summer that you can think of.
- Then make a list of all the activities you can do during the summer.
- Choose one of the activities and draw Ben doing the activity on your paper.
- Remember to add the characteristics of summer.

Talking about the Results

When you are done, display your picture in the classroom. Then answer these questions in your notebook:

- Is your drawing the same as or different from your classmates' drawings?
- How many activities are shown in the drawings? Which are repeated?
- How do you know that the photograph was taken during the summer?

How Did You Do?

For each ☺ color a ⬭.

Glossary

1.1 Key Words Unit 1

eat – *v*, to chew and swallow food
care for – *v*, to take responsibility for, look after or protect
move – *v*, to change the place, position or direction of something
feed – *v*, to give food to
grow – *v*, to increase in size; to come to life and develop; to plant

1.2 Key Words Unit 2

react – *v*, to act in response to something else
sunlight – *n*, light from the sun
pot – *n*, a rounded container of metal, baked clay or glass
shape – *n*, the outline of something; a form or a figure
size – *n*, the physical space something takes up; the length, height and width of something

1.3 Key Words Unit 3

protect – *v*, to shield from harm or keep safe; to defend
loud – *adj*, having a strong or intense sound; easy to hear
experiment – *n*, a test done carefully to show that a fact is true or to discover a new fact
communicate – *v*, to make feelings or information known to others in different ways; to write or speak
movement – *n*, the act or process of moving

1.4 Key Words Unit 4

change – *v*, to make different; alter

stretch – *v*

texture – *n*, the appearance and feel of something (rough or smooth)
recycle – *v*, to convert waste into something that can be reused
reuse – *v*, to use again or more than once

1.5 Key Words Unit 5

sky – *n*, the space between the earth and outer space
star – *n*, a huge mass of brightly burning gases in space

awake – *adj*, not asleep
asleep – *adj*, in a state of sleep; not awake
clothing – *n*, items worn to cover the body; clothes

A

absorb – *v*, to draw in and soak up
air – *n*, the invisible mixture of oxygen, nitrogen and other gases in the earth's atmosphere
artificial – *adj*, created by humans rather than nature

B

battery – *n*

branch – *n*, a part of a tree that grows from the main trunk
bright – *adj*, giving off or showing a lot of light; shining
burn – *v*, to hurt the skin with something hot

C

campfire – *n*, a fire lit outdoors in a park, forest or camp
capture – *adj*, to take something by force

category – *n*, a group of things with shared characteristics
clay – *n*, a kind of fine earth that is easily shaped when it is wet and hardens when it is dried or baked

climate – *n*, the long-term weather conditions of an area

closest – *adj*, at the shortest distance
copper – *n*, a reddish-brown metal used for electrical wiring because it is a good conductor of heat and electricity
cork – *n*, the lightweight outer bark of a tree called the cork oak
cotton – *n*, the soft, whitish fibers covering the seeds of certain plants that are made into yarn

D

daily – *adj*, happening every day
disease – *n*, a health disorder that affects the bodies of living things

E

exact – *adj*, precise, not approximate

F

farthest – *adj*, at the greatest distance
flashlight – *n*, a small light that is powered by batteries and held in the hand
flat – *adj*, even or smooth
flatten – v, to make flat or more flat
flavor – *n*, the taste of something
flower – *n*

fruit – *n*, the part of a plant that contains the seeds, such as nuts, berries or pods

G

guess – *v*, to estimate or presume something without knowing the truth

L

leaf – *n*, (plural: leaves)

leather – *n*, animal skin that has been cleaned and treated to preserve it

limb – *n*, part of the body connected to the torso, such as arms, legs or wings

listen – *v*, to hear and pay attention at the same time

N

natural – *adj*, occurring in nature; not artificial

need – *n*, something that is lacking but wanted; something that is necessary; a requirement or an obligation

nest – *n*, a structure in which birds lay their eggs and raise their young

noise – *n*, a sound, usually loud and unpleasant

nutrient – *n*, a substance that is taken in by a plant or animal in order to grow or obtain energy

O

obesity – *n*, the condition of being very overweight

P

palate – *n*, the roof of the mouth
path – *n*, a narrow road for walking along, such as in a park, a forest or the mountains
petal – *n*, one of the outer parts of a flower
photograph – *n*, a picture made from film in a camera, or a digital image
place – *n*, a space or location
plant – *n*, any living thing that makes its food from nonliving substances, has cell walls and cannot move from one place to another on its own
prohibit – *v*, to not allow

prove – *v*, to show that something is true by providing evidence
pull – *v*, to exert force by holding onto something and moving it toward you

R

root – *n*, the part of a plant that grows downward into the soil

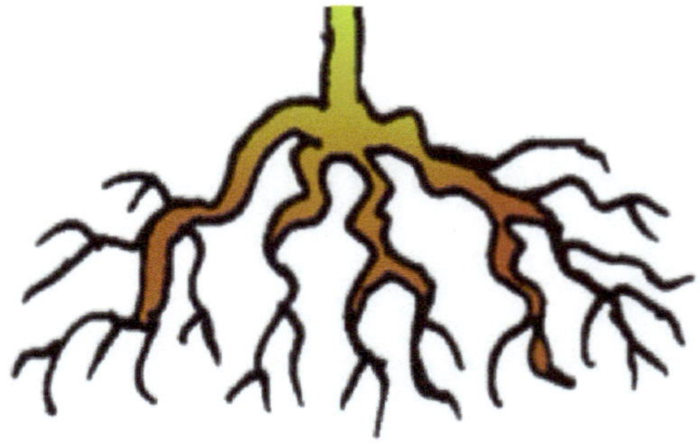

rough – *adj*, bumpy and uneven, not smooth

S

scratch – *v*, to cut or scrape with something sharp, such as nails or claws
seed – *n*, the small, hard part of a plant from which a new plant of the same type will grow

sense – *n*, sight, hearing, smell, taste or touch

shelter – *n*, something that covers or protects
shine – *v*, to give out or reflect light; to be or make bright
smooth – *adj*, not rough to the touch; even and without bumps
soak – *v*, to make people or things very wet; to take in or absorb liquid
soil – *n*, the top layer of ground that plants grow in; earth or dirt

stem – *n*, the long thin stalk of a plant that grows upward from the roots and supports the leaves, flowers and fruit
sunblock – *n*, a lotion that protects skin from sunburn and the harmful effects of the sun

T

thick – *adj*, wide, not thin
thin – *adj*, slim, not thick

transparent – *adj*, allowing light to pass through

transport – *v*, to move or carry goods or people from one place to another
trunk – *n*

U

underground – *adj*, under the surface of the earth

V

visible – *adj*, able to be seen or viewed

W

water – *n*, the liquid that falls from the sky as rain in its pure form and that has no color, taste or smell

waterproof – *adj*, not allowing water to pass through

womb – *n*, the female organ where mammals develop before they are born

wool – *n*, the soft curly hair of sheep and some other animals that is spun into yarn and made into cloth

Cutout 1

Use on page 11 (**Unit 1**).

Cutout 2

Use on page 21 (**Unit 1**).

Cutout 3

Use on page 27 (**Unit 1**).

Cutout 4

Use on page 33 (**Unit 1**).

Cutout 5

Use on page 57 (**Unit 2**).

Cutout 6

Use on page 61 (**Unit 2**).

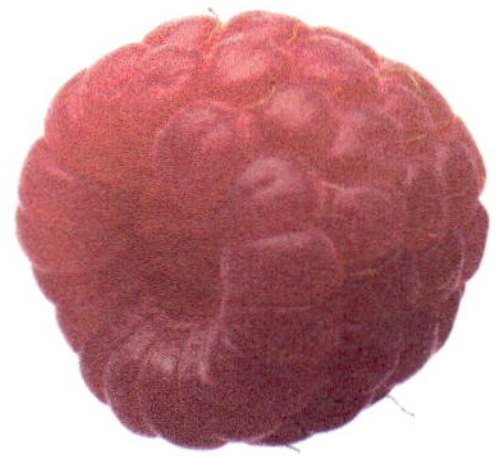

Cutout 7

Use on page 72 (**Unit 3**).

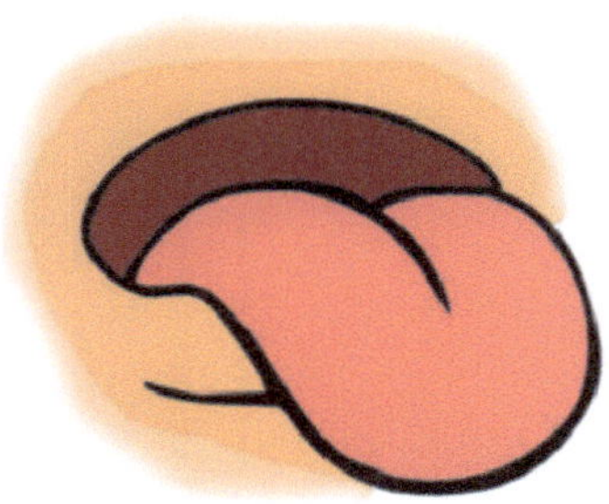
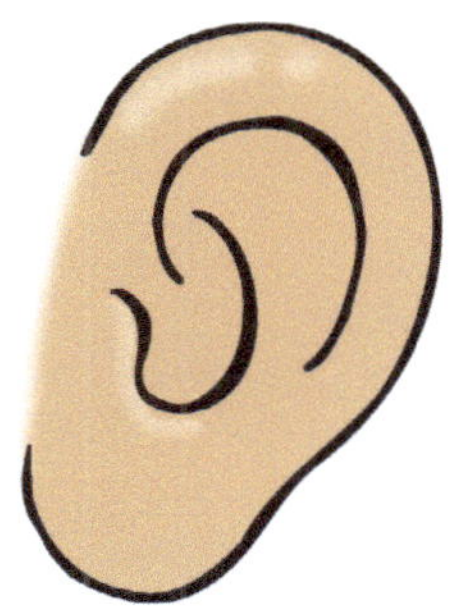
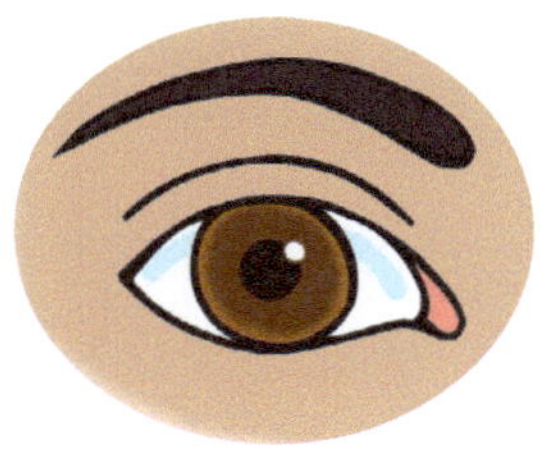

Cutout 8

Use on page 87 (**Unit 3**).

Cutout 9

Use on page 105 (**Unit 4**).

Cutout 10

Use on page 111 (**Unit 4**).

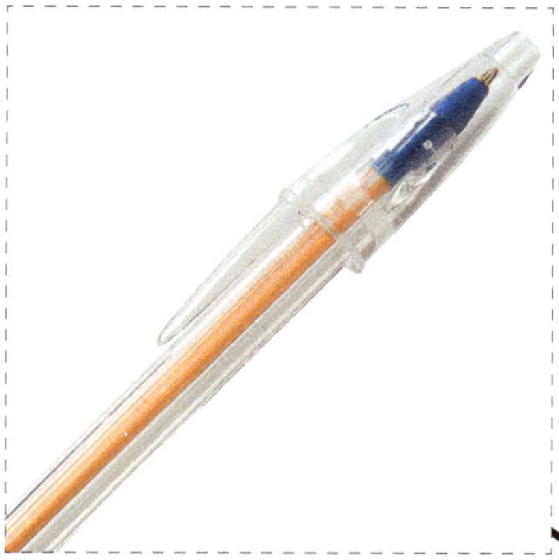

Cutout 11

Use on page 113 (**Unit 4**).

Cutout 12

Use on page 124 (**Unit 5**).

Cutout 13

Use on page 126 (**Unit 5**).

Stickers

Sticker Set 1

Use on page 9 (**Unit 1**).

Sticker Set 2

Use on page 22 (**Unit 1**).

Sticker Set 3

Use on page 37 (**Unit 1**).

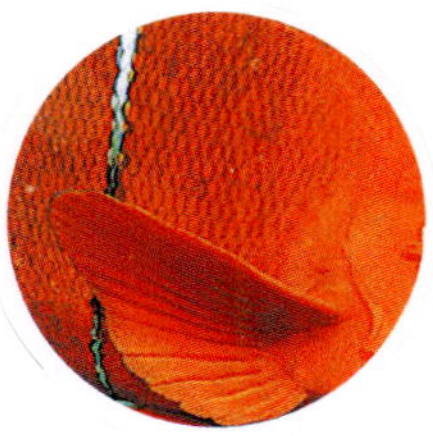

Sticker Set 4

Use on page 38 (**Unit 1**).

Sticker Set 4

Use on page 38 (**Unit 1**).

Sticker Set 5

Use on page 64 (**Unit 2**).

Sticker Set 6

Use on page 83 (**Unit 3**).

Sticker Set 7

Use on page 103 (**Unit 4**).

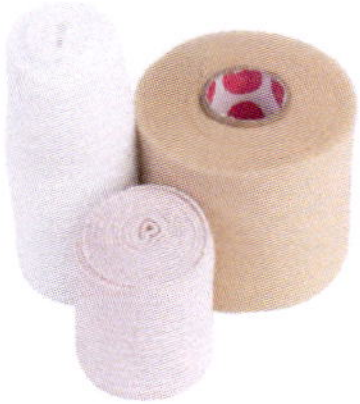

Sticker Set 8

Use on page 119 (**Unit 5**).

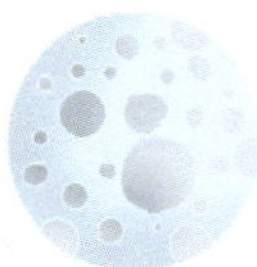

Test 1 Study Page • Summary

living things

nonliving things

Characteristics of Living Things

- growth
- reproduction
- reaction

Needs of Living Things

- to eat
- to drink water
- to breathe

domestic animals

wild animals

Sections 3, 4 and 5

3. Look at the photograph. Mark the correct answers with a ✓.

a.	☐	domestic	☐	wild
b.	☐	feet	☐	fins
c.	☐	terrestrial	☐	aquatic-terrestrial
d.	☐	viviparous	☐	oviparous
e.	☐	carnivore	☐	omnivore
f.	☐	quadruped	☐	biped
g.	☐	feathers	☐	hair
h.	☐	bigger than you	☐	smaller than you

Section 6

4. Write the names of the two mammals.

bear dolphin

glue here
glue here
glue here
glue here
glue here

Test 1 Study Page • Review

Remove, answer, and glue in your notebook.

Section 1

1. Match the pictures with the words.

living things

nonliving things

Section 2

2. Mark the correct answers with a ✔.

- ☐ Living things grow.
- ☐ Living things do not need food.
- ☐ Living things reproduce.

Name: ______________________________ Grade: __________

Characteristics of Animals

habitat

movement

reproduction

food

size

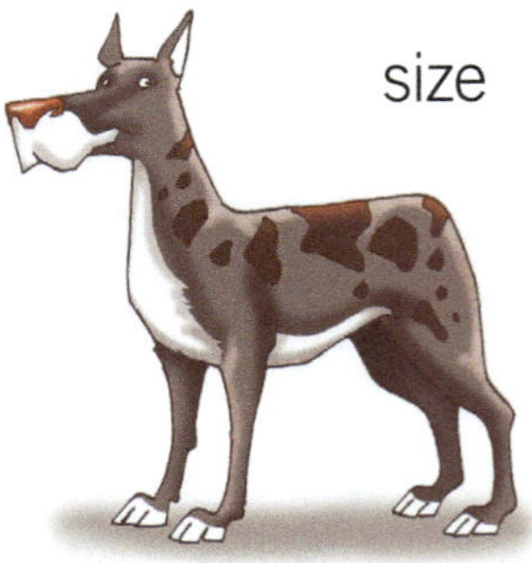

body covering

Animal Diversity

- mammals
- reptiles
- birds
- amphibians
- fish

Test 2 Study Page • Summary

Parts of a Plant

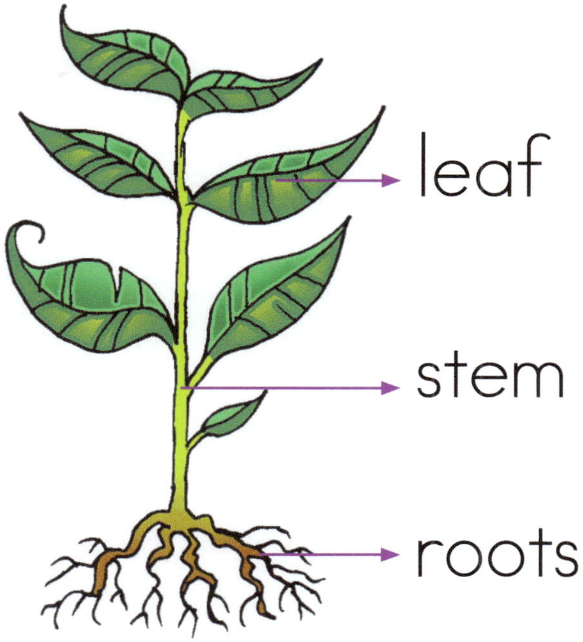

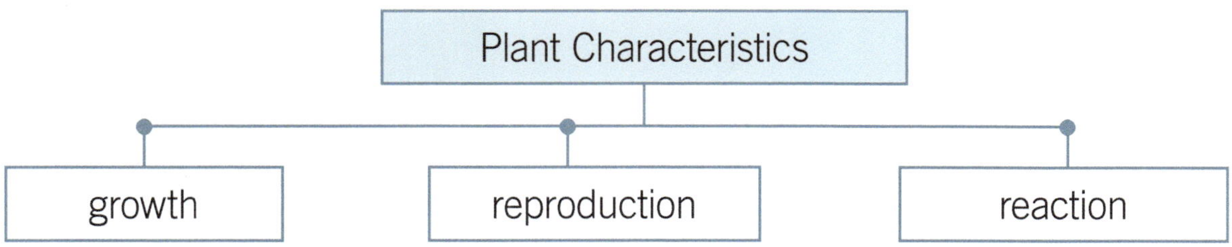

What Plants Need

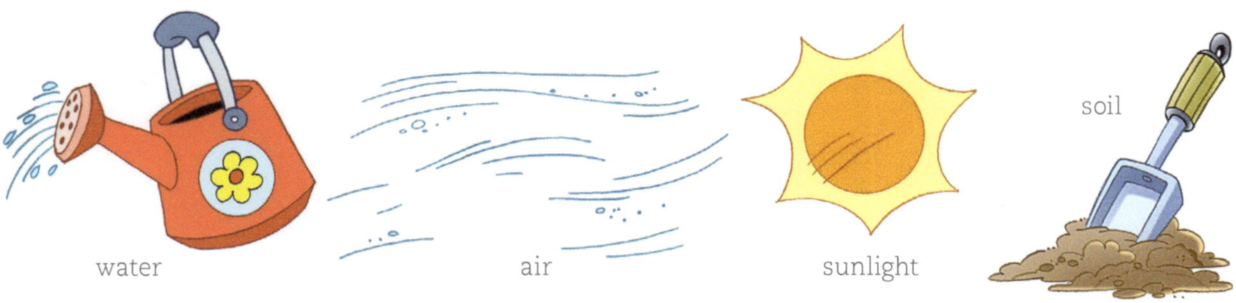

Section 3

4. Complete the sentences with the words in the box.

long	dry	size

a. Plants can by **classified** by their ______________________.

b. **Fruits** can be **fleshy** or ______________________.

c. A sunflower **seed** is a ______________________ seed.

Section 4

5. Mark with a ✔ if the plants grow in your country.

glue here

glue here

glue here

glue here

glue here

Test 2 Study Page • Review

Remove, answer, and glue in your notebook.

Section 1

1. Match each part of the **plant** with its name.

leaf roots stem

Section 2

2. Mark the **plant characteristic** with a ✔.

☐ movement ☐ reaction

3. Circle the things a plant **needs** to live.

sunlight

water

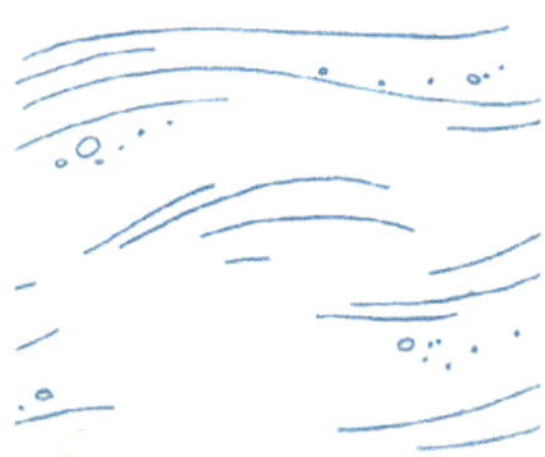

air

soil

Name: ______________________ Grade: __________

Size of plants:

- Stems / Trunks
  - soft
  - rough

- Petals
  - round
  - long

- Fruit
  - dry
  - fleshy

- Seeds
  - round
  - long

Some plants include:

The Five Senses and Related Organs

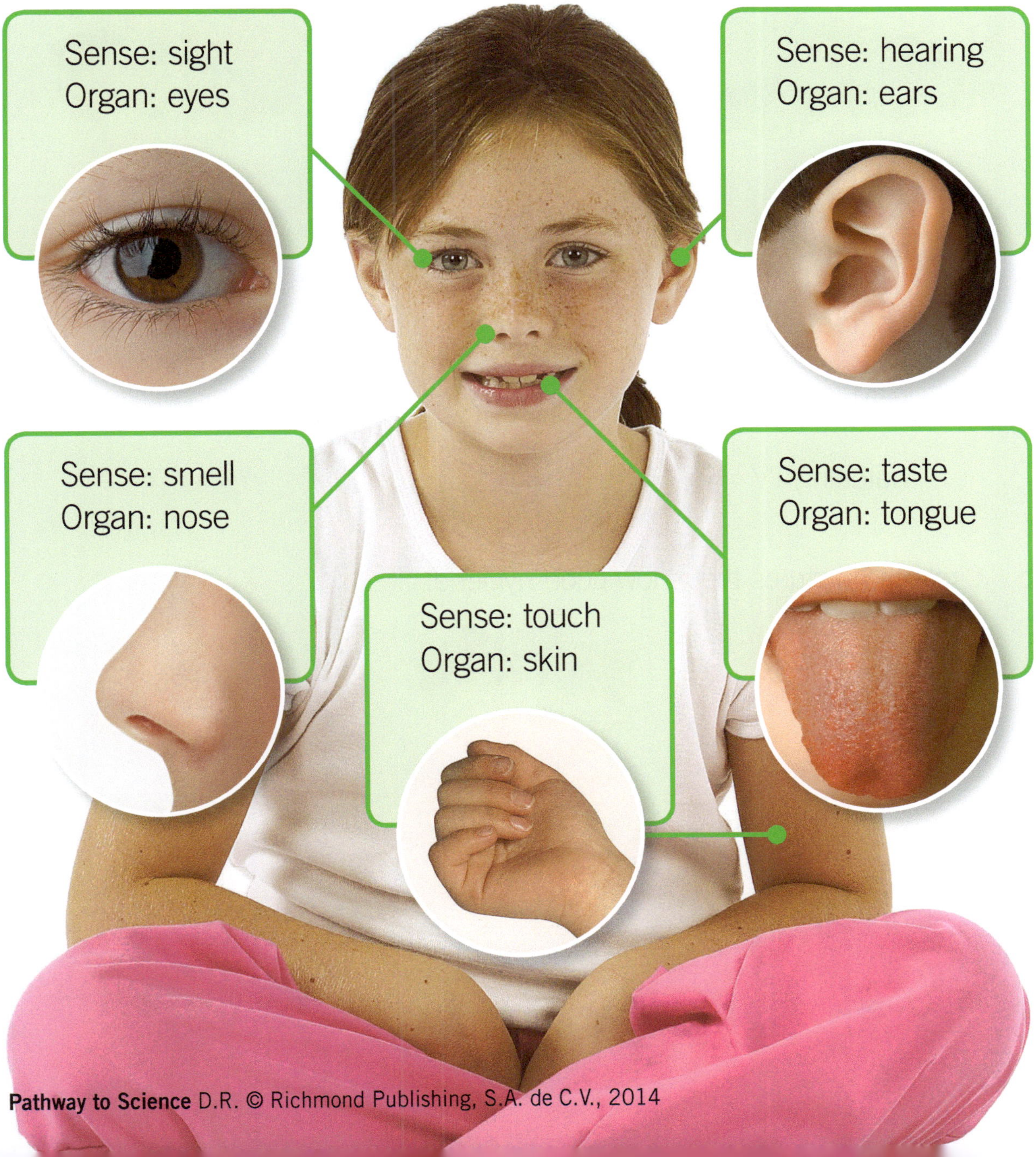

Section 3

3. Mark the **healthy foods** with a ✓.

○ ○ ○

4. Which of these activities is **exercise**? Mark the correct answer with a ✓.

☐ playing baseball

☐ watching TV

5. Circle the pictures that show good hygiene.

glue here

glue here

glue here

glue here

glue here

Test 3 Study Page • Review

Remove, answer, and glue in your notebook.

Section 1

1. What are the functions of these **organs**? Mark with a ✓.

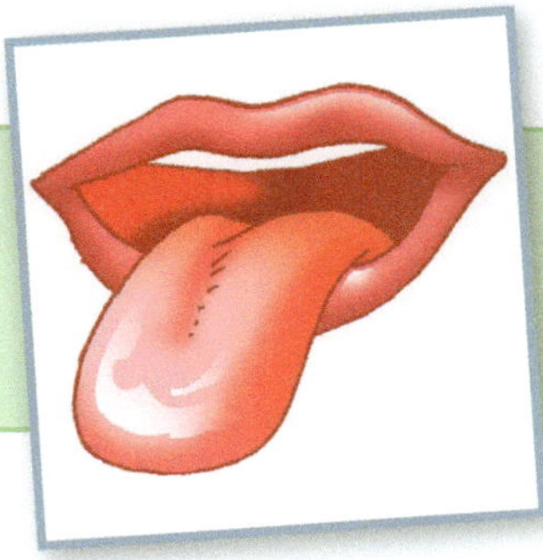

◯ to taste ◯ to smell

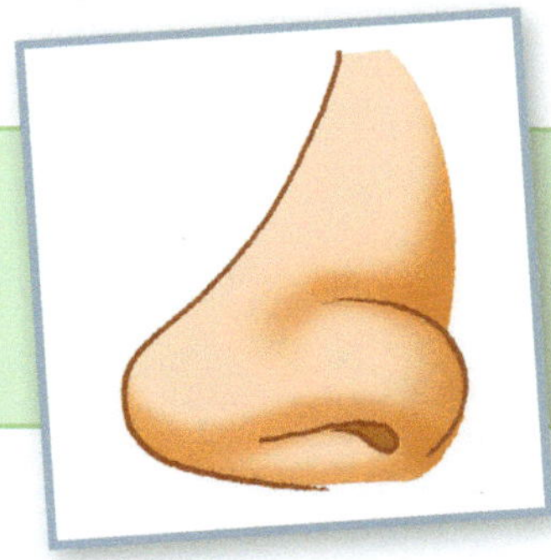

◯ to taste ◯ to smell

Section 2

2. Relate the **body parts** to the words. Use the key.

eyes ears skin

◯ rough	◯ music	◯ color
◯ thunder	◯ lightning	◯ soft

Name: ______________________ Grade: __________

Healthy Habits

Eat a balanced and varied diet.

Exercise and move for at least an hour each day.

Protect your body from illnesses with good hygiene.

Materials

natural	artificial
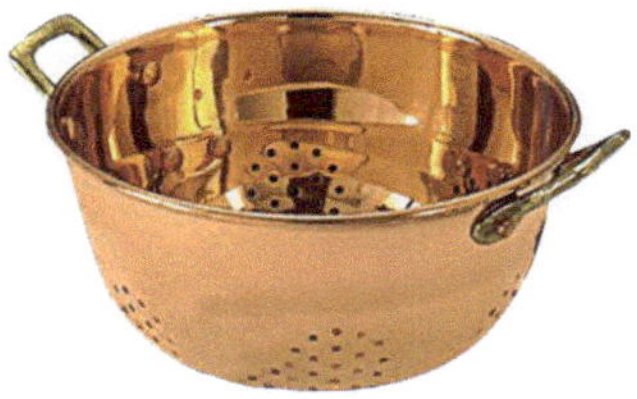	

Material Properties

hard or soft	stretchy	flexible
 diamond	 rubber band	 hose

transparent	waterproof
 glass	 garbage can

5. If you were going to make a stuffed animal, what properties would the materials need? Mark the answers with a ✓.

- [ ] hard
- [ ] stretchy
- [ ] flexible
- [ ] transparent
- [ ] waterproof
- [ ] soft

Section 3

6. What happens to a **metal spring** if you stretch it?

It changes color. It changes size. It changes shape.

7. What happens if you put **newspaper** in water? Draw what it would look like.

8. If paper is left in sunlight, how does it change? Mark with a ✓.

- [ ] It changes shape.
- [ ] It changes color.
- [ ] It changes size.

glue here

glue here

glue here

glue here

glue here

Test 4 Study Page • Review

Remove, answer, and glue in your notebook.

Section 1

1. Complete the sentences with the correct words.

cotton	materials	artificial

a. ______________ can be natural or artificial.

b. Wood and ______________ are natural materials.

c. ______________ materials are created by humans.

Section 2

2. What property do plastic and rubber have in **common**? Color.

☐ They are transparent. ☐ They are flexible. ☐ They are stretchy.

3. Why are **windows** made of glass? Mark with a ✔.

☐ Because glass is hard.

☐ Because glass is transparent.

4. What **material** would you use to make a kite? Mark with a ✔.

☐ wool ☐ plastic ☐ cardboard

Name: ______________________________ Grade: __________

How Materials Change

force

heat

light

water

Earth's Daily Cycle

Times of the Day

3. Write **D** if the animal is **diurnal** and **N** if it is **nocturnal**.

Section 2

4. When do animals **hibernate**?

- ☐ fall/autumn
- ☐ winter
- ☐ spring
- ☐ summer

5. When do most animals **reproduce**?

- ☐ fall/autumn
- ☐ winter
- ☐ spring
- ☐ summer

6. When do humans wear **warmer clothing**?

- ☐ fall/autumn
- ☐ winter
- ☐ spring
- ☐ summer

glue here
glue here
glue here
glue here
glue here

Test 5 Study Page • Review

Remove, answer, and glue in your notebook.

Section 1

1. When is it daytime? Mark with a ✔.

A When there is sunlight.

B When there are stars.

2. Number the pictures in order from 1 to 4, starting with the **morning**.

Name: ____________________ Grade: __________

The Four Seasons

summer

fall/autumn

winter

spring

Activity Card 1

Body Coverings

Remove the cards below. With a partner, play a memory game with the animals and their body coverings.

hair

hair

feathers

scales

scales

feathers

Activity Card 2

Parts of a Plant

Instructions:

- Take out the parts of the plant.
- Glue the plant together on a piece of graph paper.
- Write the name of each part of the plant.

Activity Card 3

Petal Samples

Glue the petals in the correct boxes.

long

round

Healthy Habits

What have you learned about healthy habits? Find two tokens or beans and play this game with a partner. Use the cards and coins from Activity Card 5.

Activity Card 5

Remove the cards. Fold each card in half and then glue it together.

What does a healthy breakfast consist of?	Go forward 2 spaces. Go back 1 space.	How do sports help you stay healthy?	Go forward 1 space. Go back 1 space.
Why should you brush your teeth after every meal?	Go forward 2 spaces. Go back 1 space.	Give three examples of physical activities.	Go forward 1 space. Go back 1 space.
What physical activities help take care of your body?	Go forward 1 space. Go back 1 space.	Why is it important to play outside?	Go forward 2 spaces. Go back 1 space.
Mark doesn't like to take baths or showers. What advice would you give him?	Go forward 2 spaces. Go back 1 space.	What are healthy habits?	Go forward 2 spaces. Go back 1 space.
Why are there nutritional labels on food?	Go forward 1 space. Go back 1 space.	Give five examples of healthy foods.	Go forward 2 spaces. Go back 1 space.
How can you take care of your body?	Go forward 2 spaces. Go back 1 space.	Name three actions that help take care of your body.	Go forward 1 space. Go back 1 space.

Glue the sides of the coin together. Then toss the coin to see who goes first.

Healthy Habits

Which pictures show healthy habits? Draw a ☺ or ☹ in each picture.

Activity Card 7

Materials and Their Properties

Play dominoes with the cards.

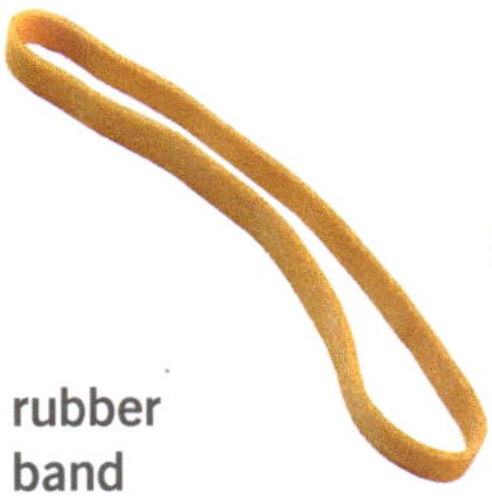
rubber band

transparent

jar

flexible

swim cap

transparent

cork

flexible

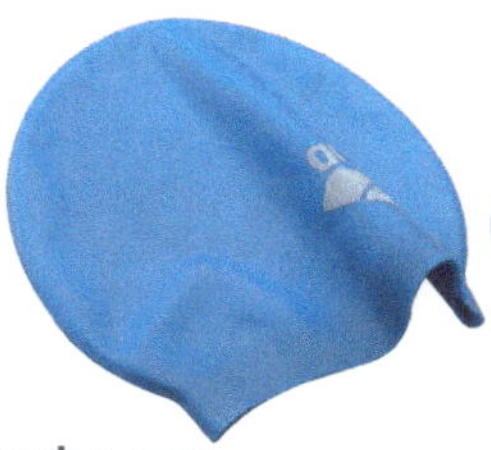
swim cap

waterproof

cork

stretchy

jar

waterproof

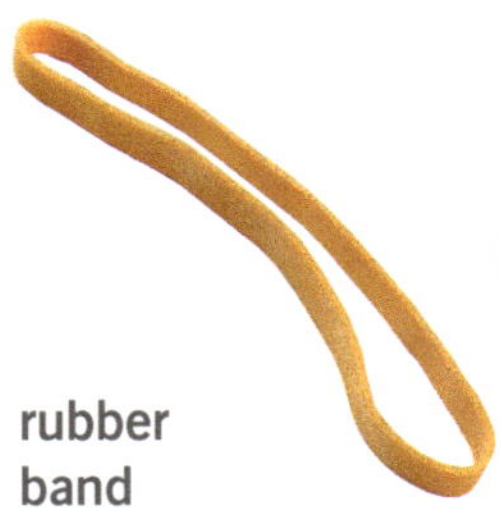
rubber band

stretchy

Activity Card 8

What Do You See When There is Sunlight?
What Do You See When There is No Sunlight?

When there is sunlight...

When there is no sunlight...

Activity Card 9

In Which Season Were You Born?

Draw a picture of the season you were born in. Include the characteristics of the climate and the clothing you wear, among other things.